TOWARDS EFFECTIVE SUBJECT LEADERSHIP IN THE PRIMARY SCHOOL

TOWARDS EFFECTIVE SUBJECT LEADERSHIP IN THE PRIMARY SCHOOL

Derek Bell
and
Ron Ritchie

Open University Press
Buckingham · Philadelphia

Open University Press
Celtic Court
22 Ballmoor
Buckingham
MK18 1XW

email: enquiries@openup.co.uk
world wide web: http://www.openup.co.uk

and
325 Chestnut Street
Philadelphia, PA 19106, USA

First Published 1999

A catalogue record of this book is available from the British Library

ISBN 0 335 20182 2 (pbk) 0 335 20183 0 (hbk)

Library of Congress Cataloging-in-Publication Data
Bell. Derek, 1950–
Towards effective subject leadership in the primary school / Derek Bell. Ron Ritchie.
p. cm.
Includes bibliographical references (p.) and index.
ISBN 0–335–20183–0 (hb). – ISBN 0–335–20182–2 (pbk)
1. Master teachers–Great Britain. 2. Mentoring in education–Great Britain. 3. Teacher participation in curriculum planning–Great Britain. 4. Elementary school teaching–Great Britain.
I. Ritchie. Ron. 1952– . II. Title.
LB2832.4.G7B45 1999
372.1102'0941–dc21

98–41546
CIP

Typeset by Graphicraft Limited, Hong Kong
Printed in Great Britain by Biddles Ltd, Guildford and King's Lynn

CONTENTS

LIST OF FIGURES

LIST OF TABLES

LIST OF CASE STUDIES

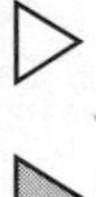

ACKNOWLEDGEMENTS

Many people, directly and indirectly, have made this book possible. We fully acknowledge their contributions and our thanks go to them all. We are forever indebted to our colleagues, students and, in particular, to the many teachers who have shared their views and practice with us in order to provide the examples of subject leadership and to help us develop the ideas that we have presented in this book. Our special thanks go to our families for their patience and support, especially to Wendy and Jill for their tolerance, continual encouragement and constructive comments on the draft material. Without these contributions this book would not have seen the light of day.

ABBREVIATIONS

CACE	Central Advisory Council for Education
DES	Department of Education and Science
DfE	Department for Education (formerly DES)
DfEE	Department for Education and Employment (formerly DfE)
HEI(s)	higher education institution(s)
HMI	Her Majesty's Inspectorate of Schools
ICT	information and communications technology
IEP(s)	individual education plan(s)
INSET	in-service education and training
ITT	initial teacher training
KS	key stage (as in KS1, KS2)
LEA	local education authority
NCC	National Curriculum Council
NGfL	National Grid for Learning
NQT	newly qualified teacher
Ofsted	Office for Standards in Education
OHP	overhead projector
PE	physical education
PoS	programme of study
PSE	personal and social education
QCA	Qualifications and Curriculum Authority
R	reception year
RE	religious education
SAT(s)	Standard Assessment Test(s)/Task(s)
SCAA	School Curriculum and Assessment Authority
SDP	school development plan
SEN	special educational needs
SENCO	special educational needs coordinator

TEC	Training and Enterprise Council
TTA	Teacher Training Agency
Y	Year (as in Y1, Y2)

INTRODUCTION

Being a coordinator (or subject leader in the future) in a primary school is and will continue to be a challenge. So much is expected of coordinators in terms of, among other things, working to develop policies and schemes of work, supporting colleagues as well as monitoring and evaluating the teaching and learning that is taking place in the subject area (or frequently the areas) for which they are responsible. The challenge is all the greater because, for the vast majority of coordinators, the responsibilities they undertake are in addition to their roles as full-time class teachers. Furthermore, the contribution that coordinators make to the running of their schools, the quality and standards of the teaching and learning that occur and the overall effectiveness of their schools has come under closer scrutiny in recent years because of increased accountability.

Thus, taking on the post of coordinator can be a daunting task even for experienced teachers, especially when, as is often the case, the area of responsibility is for subjects other than those that formed the major part of their training. It is not uncommon for someone, for example, with a degree in English to be the coordinator for science. This situation in itself provides a particular challenge, which is then added to by the demands arising from other unfamiliar issues relating to leadership and management and the development of the skills needed to meet all the responsibilities of the post. For someone new to the post of coordinator there are many questions to be answered, for example: Is the policy and scheme of work appropriate and up to date? Is everyone using the scheme of work effectively? What changes could the coordinator introduce to improve children's learning throughout the school? Which colleagues need help and how can they be supported effectively? In what ways can difficult situations be resolved? Do the resources need updating and making more accessible? In what other ways might the subject be developed in the school over the next few years? What support does the coordinator need and how might it be provided? How can everything be fitted in?

It is these questions, amongst others, that we have addressed in this book, which aims to provide a framework for reflection on, and analysis of, the complex process of curriculum leadership and coordination in primary schools. We have taken a generic approach to look at issues, such as the changing roles and responsibilities (Part I), planning for teaching and learning (Part II), working with colleagues and others (Part III), managing resources (Part IV) and bringing about school improvement (Part V), that have to be addressed by all coordinators whatever their particular area of responsibility. We have, however, focused on the particular challenges of those coordinators who are responsible for individual subjects within the curriculum. Most importantly we have based the book on two assumptions:

1 The aim of effective curriculum leadership and coordination, regardless of subject area, is to provide the best possible learning opportunities for the children in a school at any given time.
2 The post of coordinator is a rapidly evolving and complex one which requires extending professional and personal development into new areas, in particular those of leadership and management.

It is partly because of the latter assumption that we propose to adopt the term subject leader throughout the book. As we argue in Chapter 1, the changing nature of the post of coordinator and the increasing demands on those who are trying to implement it require a more proactive stance than perhaps has been recognized previously and this is better reflected in the term subject leader.

This book, therefore, aims to examine the post of subject leader in primary schools in the light of the four key areas (strategic direction and development; teaching and learning; leading and managing staff; efficient and effective deployment of staff and resources) defined by the National Standards for Subject Leadership (TTA 1998a). It combines existing research data and new material gathered by the authors to present the underpinning principles and to analyse the complex set of roles and responsibilities. Most importantly it provides practical advice for subject leaders working in their schools and is illustrated by a series of case studies and tasks that are addressed directly to subject leaders. In doing so we emphasize the qualities of leadership, children's learning, professional development and collaboration.

Although we have set the book out in parts in order to focus on particular aspects of the work of subject leaders, many of the ideas are interlinked. Part I sets out an overview of the development of the post (Chapter 1) and provides an outline of what the post involves. We consider the characteristics of leadership in Chapter 2 and then start to examine how the skills might be applied in school (Chapter 3). The importance of taking a longer term view and the development of good professional relationships are particularly emphasized.

Part II focuses on teaching and learning and explores ways in which subject leaders can contribute to improvements in the classroom (Chapter 4). Planning for effective teaching and learning across the whole school is considered in Chapter 5 while assessment issues are discussed in Chapter 6.

Part III considers the importance of other people as partners in the education of children and examines ways of working effectively with them. Chapter 7 looks at the professional relationships that need to be developed while Chapters 8 and 9 concentrate on ways of supporting and working with colleagues both on an individual basis and as a group.

Part IV examines issues concerning resources, including time, that are always limited and have to be carefully managed in order to make effective use of them. Chapter 10 considers the physical resources such as equipment, books and the school environment. The vexed question of time and how to make the most of it is taken up in Chapter 11.

Part V returns to some overarching themes including monitoring and evaluation (Chapter 12) and the management of change (Chapter 13). Both of these chapters examine the issues raised in the context of inspections and the development of excellence in schools. Chapter 14 tries to draw out the lessons we have learnt about the developing roles of subject leaders in the context of their school and in relation to the head teacher and other colleagues. In the last analysis subject leaders cannot do everything by themselves. It is the concerted effort of everyone in a school that will bring about the best possible learning opportunities for the children at any given time, but it is subject leaders who have the responsibility to make it happen in their subjects.

Part I

CHANGING RESPONSIBILITIES AND ROLES

1

COORDINATOR OR SUBJECT LEADER?

Introduction

Subject leaders have a key position in the organization, development and management of the curriculum in primary schools. Without doubt it is not easy to carry out such a complex job effectively but where subject leaders are successful they have a significant influence on the quality of teaching and learning that takes place (e.g. Ofsted 1996a). The requirements of the subject leader are demanding, involving those issues that might be described as curriculum matters as well as those relating to leadership and management. In most primary schools the situation is further complicated by the fact that clear demarcations are virtually non-existent, with everyone having responsibility for some aspect of the curriculum; the management roles often overlap and conflict with other areas of responsibility, most notably that of being a class teacher; and the subject boundaries are often less well defined than in secondary schools. In this chapter we trace the development of the post of subject leader and explore the scope of such positions in the context of current developments in primary schools.

From consultant to subject leader: an historical perspective

The importance of subject leadership is particularly highlighted in the current climate, encompassing among other things the overall drive to raise standards, Office for Standards in Education (Ofsted) inspections, statutory National Curriculum and assessment requirements, changing role of local education authorities (LEAs) and the development of a national framework of professional standards for teachers. Yet the idea of teachers in primary schools having responsibility, however informally, for providing a degree of specialist expertise in support of their colleagues is not new. The Board of Education handbook (1905: 17), for example, suggested that head teachers distribute work to 'assign instructions to those members of staff who have special knowledge' of particular subjects, while the Ministry of Education Handbook (1959: 94) encourages head teachers to make use of 'staff's special interests and knowledge [and get staff] to seek specialist help from each other when it is available'.

The Plowden Report (CACE 1967), which used the term 'consultant', and Her Majesty's Inspectorate of Schools (HMI; DES 1978) 10 years later started to define wider responsibilities and to establish the link between effective curriculum coordination and the quality of the learning that was taking place. This extended notion of what coordinators might do in their schools continued to develop throughout the 1970s and 1980s to the extent that:

> The Government believe that all primary teachers should be equipped to take a particular responsibility for one aspect of the curriculum (such as science, mathematics or music), to act as consultants to their colleagues on that aspect and, where appropriate, to teach it to classes other than their own.
>
> (DES 1983: paragraph 33)

This intention became a reality when, in 1987, new structures and duties for all teaching staff were agreed, which included the requirement that each teacher in primary schools would be expected to take responsibility for a curriculum area (DES 1988).

The introduction of the National Curriculum for England and Wales in the following year was accompanied by guidance (NCC 1989) which strengthened the case for curriculum leadership and set out some areas of responsibility for those undertaking the task:

> Where possible, teachers should share responsibility for curriculum leadership to include:
>
> - detailing schemes of work in the light of the Programmes of Study;
> - working alongside colleagues;
> - arranging school-based INSET;
> - evaluating curriculum development;
> - liaising with other schools;
> - keeping 'up-to-date' in the particular subject;
> - managing resources.
>
> (NCC 1989:12)

In the 1990s the significance of teachers with some kind of specialist role continued to be a key element in debates about the nature of the primary curriculum (e.g. Alexander *et al.* 1992). Ofsted described coordinators as managers stating:

> teachers who are subject managers for the whole school (co-ordinators is too limited a description) can be expected to:

- develop a clear view of the nature of their subject and its contribution to the wider curriculum;
- provide advice and documentation to help teachers teach the subject and interrelate its constituent elements;
- play a major part in organising the teaching and the resources of the subjects so that statutory requirements are covered;

> . . . [and] to contribute to the overall evaluation of work in their subject against agreed criteria, to evaluate standards of achievements and to identify trends and patterns in pupils' performance.
>
> (Ofsted 1994: paras 37, 38)

The importance of the need for a whole school perspective when undertaking the work of coordinator was emphasized by Ofsted in the framework for inspection:

> Inspectors need to establish whether the governing body has developed a strategic view of the school's development and the extent to which the headteacher (and senior management team where applicable) provides positive leadership which gives a firm steer to the school's work. The same perspective should apply to the way coordinators carry out their responsibilities.
>
> (Ofsted 1995a:102)

More recently all the elements of a coordinator's job have been encompassed in the Teacher Training Agency (TTA 1998a) standards for subject leaders which identify the core purpose of subject leadership as the need 'to provide professional leadership and management for a subject to secure high quality teaching, effective use of resources, and improved standards of learning and achievement for all pupils'. The standards go on to describe the 'key areas of subject leadership' as 'strategic direction and development of the subject', 'teaching and learning', 'leading and managing staff' and 'efficient and effective deployment of staff and resources'. While there are differences in emphasis and level of detail, the requirements set out by Ofsted and the TTA are largely in keeping with earlier research (e.g. Campbell 1985; Morrison 1986; Stow and Foxman 1988; Bell 1992) into the role of the coordinator. Similarly materials (e.g. Davies 1995; Harrison 1995; West 1995) that aim to provide support and advice for coordinators refer to broadly the same areas of responsibility. Thus there would appear to be some degree of consensus as to what the post of subject leader might involve (Bell 1996a).

Subject leader or coordinator: what's in a name?

Although there has been a great deal of convergence as to the nature of the post there is still some ambiguity in the terminology that is used to describe the person undertaking the it. A variety of terms have been used over the years such as: specialist (Morrison 1986), consultant (CACE 1967), post of

Case Study 1.1 A 'coordinator'

Margaret has worked in her school for 10 years and has had responsibility for three different curriculum areas and is currently responsible for geography and history. The school was built in the mid-1960s with a semi-open plan layout and has 220 children from Y1 to Y6 divided into eight classes.

Margaret wrote a policy two years ago and finished revising the scheme of work 12 months ago. She is quite satisfied that most of her colleagues are using the scheme of work and that the children seem to be enjoying the topics they are doing. Although money has been tight Margaret has managed to get together a suitable collection of resources in the form of books and artefacts which individual teachers supplement when they do particular topics.

Margaret feels that, now things are running smoothly, she is on top of her job as coordinator and, apart from reviewing the policy, perhaps next year, does not need to worry too much about these two subjects.

responsibility (ASE 1981), postholder (Campbell 1985), coordinator (DES 1975 1982; Blenkinsop 1991), subject manager (Ofsted 1994, West 1995) and subject leader (TTA 1998a). Each term brings with it different impressions as to the way in which the post might be perceived and carried out. The term coordinator is perhaps the most widely used, but subject leader is the form that has been adopted by the TTA (1998a) for the national standards. It is worth considering therefore what each of these two terms might imply in order to clarify the situation. We can do this by looking at Case Studies 1.1 and 1.2.

Consideration of the two case studies indicates that both individuals have the potential to do exactly the same job in similar ways. Margaret, however, although she has provided the basis for sound teaching, is not looking for ways in which to monitor what is happening nor does she appear to be looking for ways to improve things. Di, on the other hand, is trying to move things forward and is thinking about different ways in which she can support her colleagues, help them to extend their teaching and to monitor how they are getting on. She is also trying to explore ways in which she can improve the PE that is available in the school by involving the local sports clubs. Neither Margaret nor Di would argue that things are perfect, but Di is motivated to try to do different things while Margaret seems to concentrate on maintaining the status quo.

In Table 1.1 we have tried to summarize the distinctions between the two approaches described in the case studies. The term coordinator tends to imply a position that is passive and reactive to the responsibilities and opportunities that present themselves. The term subject leader on the other hand suggests a more proactive approach that anticipates events, plans for

Case Study 1.2 A 'subject leader'

Di has been responsible for physical education (PE) in her school for the last one and a half years, having been in charge of geography for three years before that. Her school is in Victorian buildings but is next to some playing fields that the school can use in addition to the yard. Although somewhat reluctant initially to take on PE, Di is now very keen to make sure that all children benefit from the opportunities that are available. Di says that after going on a course for PE coordinators run by the LEA, she realized that she could improve the PE in her school and now has many ideas about what could be done with some planning and encouragement. The course helped her develop a vision of how PE could develop over the next few years.

The equipment available for PE is rather basic and limited. However, after completing an audit of what everyone did in PE and how they felt about it, Di set about working on a policy and scheme of work. Two colleagues collaborated with her on this task. The results were discussed and agreed at a staff meeting. The majority of her colleagues seemed 'comfortable' with the approach and shared Di's aspirations for the subject. Every class teacher is now using the scheme and Di has provided support in the form of written materials with ideas for activities and has carried out some demonstration lessons for all the staff.

Di feels that there is a long way to go and is monitoring progress by offering to help her colleagues (especially those least confident with PE) to plan lessons. Although this is a start she would like to find better ways of monitoring and, providing the head teacher agrees, would like to spend some time working alongside her colleagues during their lessons. She would also like to introduce a wider range of PE activities for the children and has approached some of the local sports clubs for help.

improvements and creates opportunities in order to increase the effectiveness of teaching in the subject and pupils' learning across the whole school.

We must emphasize that we are not suggesting that someone who is designated a coordinator does not, nor cannot, do the things a subject leader does. For many taking on the responsibility for a curriculum area, however, the coordinator approach is perhaps the most comfortable one to take and may have advantages in the early stages of taking up the post in trying to evaluate the situation. Unfortunately, if this view is maintained it will be limiting and result in the maintenance of the status quo rather than bringing about change. Evidence from earlier work (Bell, 1990; 1992, Edwards 1993) indicates that the general perception of coordinators in the past has been of this restricted nature. In order to move things on and bring about the desired improvements in quality and standards the more proactive approach implied by the term subject leader is required. This acknowledges

Table 1.1 Coordinator v subject leader

In the past coordinators have tended to:	Subject leaders aim to:
• be reactive	• be proactive
• focus on the current situation	• be forward looking and innovative
• avoid conflict at all costs	• recognize the potential of conflict
• respond to events	• anticipate events
• take up opportunities as they appear	• create opportunities
• accept current situation uncritically	• challenge current practices
• be class focused	• be whole school focused
• have a narrow, local and limited perspective	• have broad local and national perspective
• underplay expertise	• enhance expertise
• feel subject knowledge is not essential	• recognize value of subject knowledge
• support colleagues	• develop colleagues
• carry out maintenance tasks	• initiate and carry out developmental tasks
• make ad hoc decisions based on immediate needs	• engage in action planning based on short, medium and long term needs
• be reluctant to set targets	• define goals and set targets at whole school level
• be individualistic	• foster collaborative working
• monitor in an ad hoc manner	• monitor systematically

the subject leader to be an agent of change involved in: maintenance and development; organization and delivery; planning and implementation; and monitoring and evaluation. In this book we aim to provide support for this extended view and set out practical advice on how to bring about the necessary changes now asked of schools. It is for this reason that we have adopted the term subject leader throughout.

Task 1.1

Look at Case Studies 1.1 and 1.2 again. With whom, Margaret or Di, do you identify most closely? Reflect on the way other coordinators in your school carry out their jobs – with which of the two models do they have most parallels? If you find yourself identifying with the 'coordinator', consider the opportunities and threats that the subject leader approach offers to you.

Defining responsibilities, roles and tasks

It is quite clear that in a comparatively short time the position of subject leader has changed from being a relatively uncommon feature in many primary schools to one that is seen as central to the effective functioning of primary schools. Subject leaders thus have a key part to play in raising standards and enhancing quality in all primary schools. It is important, however, to understand what is involved in terms of the responsibilities, roles and tasks that a subject leader undertakes. Making this clear is not always easy because on the one hand the outcome could be a daunting list of items somewhat similar the TTA standards (TTA 1998a) while on the other a few general statements are very little help and can lead to confusion.

Furthermore the terms 'responsibility', 'role' and 'task' are often used in different ways by writers and others. In particular we would suggest that the use of the phrase 'the role of the subject leader' is misleading and implies that there is a single role to be played. Nothing could be further from the truth. The subject leader carries out a variety of roles, often at the same time, thus we refer to 'the roles of the subject leader' and describe the work of the subject leader in terms of:

- the post of subject leader, which refers to the position in the school and encompasses all aspects of the work;
- the responsibilities of subject leader, which set out the things that subject leaders need to make happen and should be agreed as part of a job description alongside some annual targets;
- the roles of the subject leader, which define the functions that are undertaken, in order to achieve the various aspects of the post in relation its overall purpose, context, and the interrelationships involved;
- the tasks, which are the specific activities that subject leaders need to do in order to meet their responsibilities on a day to day, week to week basis. It is worth remembering that these have to be carried out in addition to being a class teacher.

The post of subject leader

The overall purpose of the subject leader is to contribute to school improvement and increase standards through the provision of high quality teaching and the best possible learning opportunities for children. In order to bring this about the subject leader has to lead and manage the curriculum itself, the demands for accountability and the need for quality. In addition external developments have to be catered for, including changes to the National Curriculum, new initiatives such as the introduction of the literacy and numeracy hours, Ofsted inspections, and publication of Standard Assessment Test (SAT) results. All of these demands have to be met in the context of school based factors such as resources, the expertise and attitudes of colleagues, and the time available. It is also worth highlighting that the requirements and perceptions of the actual post held and the experience of its holder can differ quite markedly depending on which subject is being led. Subject leaders responsible for English and maths are often regarded as having a higher status and thus given higher priority. Science, the third core

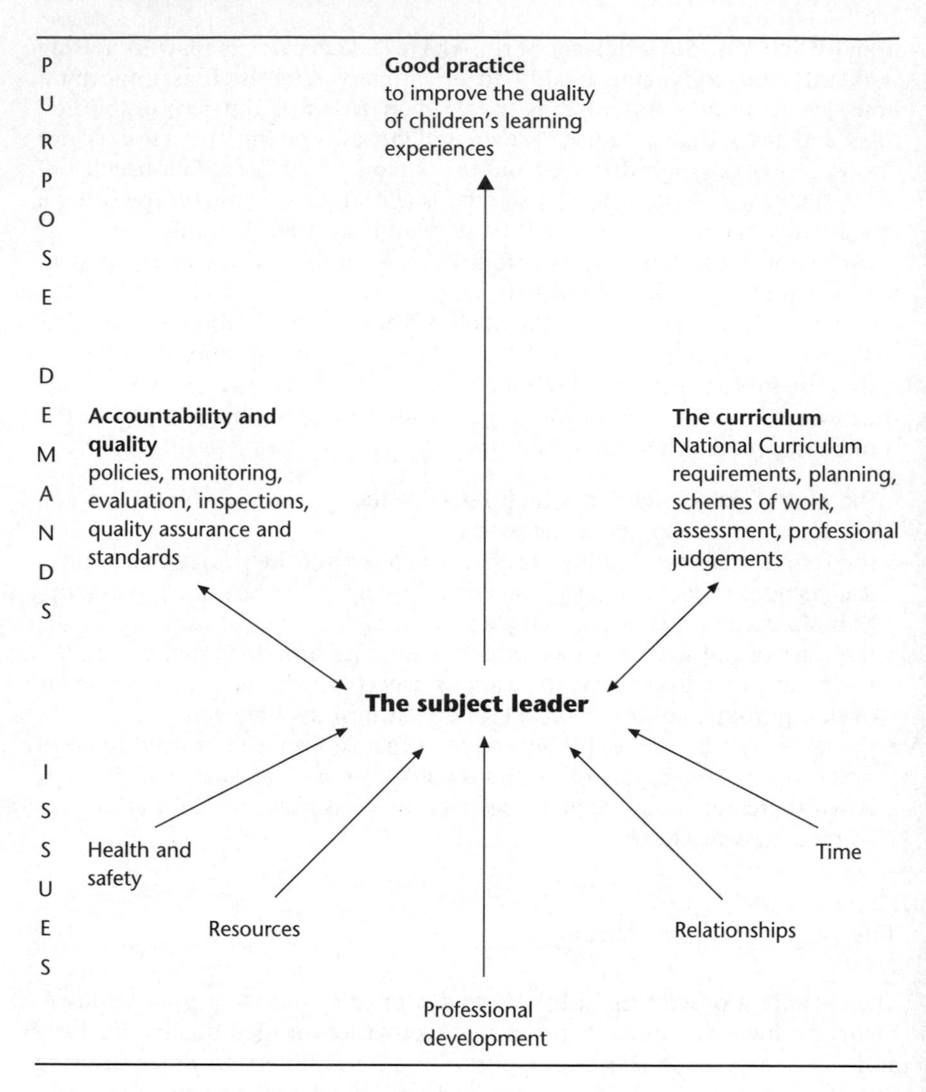

Figure 1.1 The post of subject leader

subject in the National Curriculum for England and Wales, may in turn be given higher status than the remaining subject areas, which are designated as the foundation subjects. It is this overall context we have represented in Figure 1.1.

Responsibilities of subject leaders

Every school is unique, therefore the precise demands on individual subject leaders will differ from school to school, within each school and with time.

It is helpful, however, to provide an overview of the post showing how the responsibilities, roles and tasks are linked. We have done this in Table 1.2, which reflects the four key areas of subject leadership (TTA 1998a) as:

1. strategic direction and development of the subject requiring vision, setting of targets and recognizing the need for change;
2. teaching and learning, focusing on ways in which these can be improved thereby raising quality and standards for children and their achievements;
3. leading and managing people working towards a culture of collaboration, cooperation and partnership as well as the development of personal and professional expertise;
4. managing resources, aiming to ensure the availability, efficient and effective use of time, personnel and materials.

Table 1.2 provides a list of items for which the subject leader might be responsible in each of the four areas. The list is, paradoxically, neither comprehensive in stating that every subject leader should undertake all of these items nor is it exhaustive in suggesting that these are the only things that will be required of a subject leader. For example, many subject leaders do not have responsibility for a budget, as this is often dealt with directly by the head teacher. Thus it is essential that each subject leader negotiates with their head teacher which aspects of the post they are responsible for and which are to be taken on by someone else. Essentially this requires agreement on a job description, which we look at in more detail in Chapter 7. It is important to stress at this point that a suitably negotiated job description not only identifies the responsibilities of the subject leader but it also provides a basis for discussions designed to plan for the subject leader's own professional development in order to equip them to meet the demands of the post.

The roles of subject leaders

In meeting their responsibilities, subject leaders have to adopt of variety of roles involving the use of a combination of curriculum and interpersonal skills (Campbell 1985). The complex interaction of the roles was recognized by Bell (1992, 1993) who proposed a dynamic and proactive model, requiring the subject leader to:

- initiate the development of [subject] teaching and learning in the school;
- facilitate the development of [subject] teaching and learning in the school;
- coordinate the development of [subject] teaching and learning in the school;
- evaluate the development of [subject] teaching and learning in the school;
- educate others in order to help them develop [subject] teaching and learning in the school.

Bentley and Watts (1994) extended this model to show three major dimensions running through the work of the subject leader, each carrying with it a

Table 1.2 Responsibilities, roles and tasks of subject leaders (based on National Standards for Subject Leaders, TTA 1998a)

Core purpose: to provide professional leadership and management for a subject to secure high quality teaching, effective use of resources and improved standards of learning and achievement for all pupils within the context of the school's overall aims and policies and commitment to high achievement and effective teaching and learning.

Key areas are	*Responsibilities to*	*Roles involved*	*Tasks include*
Strategic direction and development of the subject – to develop and implement subject policies, plans, targets and practices.	• develop and implement policies and practices • create and maintain a climate of positive attitudes and confidence in teaching • establish shared understanding of the importance and role of the subject • identify and plan for supporting underachieving pupils • analyse and interpret appropriate data, research and inspection evidence • establish short, medium and long term plans for development and resourcing of the subject • monitor progress in achieving plans and targets and evaluate effects to inform further improvement	leader policymaker initiator planner advocate negotiator analyst decisionmaker delegator evaluator	• auditing the subject • analysing and evaluating data and evidence • talking with the head teacher, colleagues and governors • seeking appropriate advice • agreeing aims, targets, criteria for success and deadlines • preparing action plans • documenting policies and plans

Teaching and learning – to secure and sustain effective teaching of the subject, evaluate the quality of teaching and standards of pupils' achievements and set targets for improvement.	• ensure curriculum coverage, continuity and progression for **all** pupils • ensure teachers understand and communicate objectives and sequence of teaching and learning • provide guidance on teaching and learning methods to meet pupil and subject needs • ensure development of literacy, numeracy and ICT skills through the subject • establish and implement policies and practices for assessing, recording and reporting • ensure information on pupils' achievement is used to secure progress • set expectations for staff and pupils and evaluate progress and achievement of **all** pupils • evaluate teaching, identify good practice and act to improve the quality of teaching • ensure development of pupils' individual and collaborative study skills • ensure teachers are aware of subject's contribution to pupil's understanding of citizenship • ensure teachers can recognize and deal with racial stereotyping • establish partnership and involvement of parents • develop links with the community, business and industry	adviser planner educator consultant coordinator learner subject 'expert'	• preparing and documenting schemes of work, assessments, records and reports • talking with and advising colleagues on activities and lessons • suggesting ideas and starting points • supporting knowledge and understanding • talking to outside contacts • putting up displays and promoting the subject • keeping up to date with new ideas • check links with other areas of the curriculum

Table 1.2 (Cont'd)

Key areas are	*Responsibilities to*	*Roles involved*	*Tasks include*
Leading and managing staff – to provide to all those with involvement in the teaching or support of the subject, the support, challenge, information and development necessary to sustain motivation and secure improvement in teaching.	• help staff achieve constructive working relationships with pupils • establish expectations and constructive working relationships among staff • sustain motivation of themselves and colleagues • appraise staff, if appropriate • audit training needs • lead professional development and coordinate provision • ensure trainees and NQTs are supported to achieve appropriate standards • enable colleagues to achieve expertise in subject teaching • work with SENCO to develop IEPs • ensure head teacher, senior managers and governors are well informed	leader manager motivator negotiator collaborator delegator diplomat mediator listener confidant critical friend educator learner	• planning, arranging and running INSET • working alongside colleagues in classrooms • listening to colleagues • keeping colleagues up to date • presenting subject to governors
Efficient and effective deployment of staff and resources – to identify appropriate resources for the subject and ensure that they are used efficiently, effectively and safely.	• establish and advise on **all** resource needs and allocate subject resources efficiently • advise on the best use of colleagues • ensure effective and efficient management and organization of learning resources including ICT • maintain existing resources and explore opportunities to develop and incorporate new ones • use accommodation to create a stimulating environment • ensure a safe working and learning environment	manager organizer planner provider facilitator technician	• selecting and ordering materials and equipment • organizing storage and making sure resources are accessible • demonstrating use of equipment • finding out about new resources • monitoring the budget • auditing resources • finding alternative ways of using the environment • assessing risks with equipment and activities

series of roles. Thus Bentley and Watts envisaged the work of the subject leader in terms of:

- working with other people as an educator, adviser and facilitator;
- the subject as a researcher and developer;
- the whole school as a manager, planner and evaluator.

There are, however, dangers in trying to fix a model that lists every possible role in which a subject leader might become engaged, not least the fact that the model becomes too complicated and is not helpful. Rather we need a framework in which it is possible to identify roles as they develop and allows scope for the model to evolve as time and place change. In Table 1.2 we have attempted to set out the variety and range of roles subject leaders may undertake but do not regard the list as being fixed. On the contrary we would suggest that the number of combinations is almost endless.

Subject leader tasks

The range of tasks carried out by subject leaders is extensive. Table 1.2 provides an overview of the major tasks linked to the areas of responsibility considered above. Drawing up such lists is relatively easy but the translation of them into practice is significantly more difficult as a small scale study from our research (Bell 1997) illustrates.

Table 1.3 shows how the 20 subject leaders in this study spent their time on differing tasks related to their post during the four weeks of the study. On average the subject leaders in this study spent between four and five hours per week carrying out tasks that were considered to be part of their role in addition to teaching their class. The time spent ranged from as little as 48 minutes to 10 hours 15 minutes, the major proportion (44 per cent) of time being taken up with activities that related to professional development of the coordinator. This, however, included two hours per week attending a course for curriculum coordination they were undertaking at the time and is

Table 1.3 Time (in minutes) spent on different categories of tasks

	Average time per week	*Range of time spent on each category of task*	*Number of subject leaders not doing the tasks (n = 20)*
Resources	64	0–279	1
Professional development	127	0–690	3
Supporting colleagues	24	0–85	2
Planning	61	0–163	3
Evaluation	13	0–65	7
Overall	289	48–615	

therefore not typical of the whole year. Resources (22 per cent) and planning (21 per cent) were next, with the provision of support for colleagues (8 per cent) and evaluation (5 per cent) accounting for the remaining time.

It is dangerous to generalize from such a small scale study but it is clear that there is a wide range of practice with many subject leaders being unable to spend so much time on their tasks. Perhaps the most outstanding piece of evidence from the findings presented here is the imbalance of time that is given to different aspects of the coordinators' work. As Table 1.3 shows, the time spent on supporting colleagues and evaluation activities is very much less than that taken up with tasks related to other aspects of the coordinator's job. Although the amount of time in itself cannot be taken as the only factor, this major imbalance suggests that these two areas, which should have a significant impact on the quality of the curriculum and the teaching and learning in a primary school, are being neglected. Concern about these aspects was noted by Ofsted (1995a:103): 'a test of effective leadership and management is the commitment to monitoring and evaluating teaching and the curriculum and to taking action to sustain and improve their quality.' Subject leaders need to be clear about what they actually need to do in order to achieve the targets they set themselves. This requires an appreciation of the balance of the tasks undertaken and the cooperation of their colleagues in order to use what time is available more effectively.

Task 1.2

Use Table 1.2 as a starting point and identify which tasks you carry out as a subject leader. List any additional ones and allocate them to the appropriate responsibilities. Which responsibilities of subject leadership are you covering at present? Which areas do you think you need to develop?

Making an impact on children's learning

One of the key areas of responsibility for a subject leader is to make an impact on children's learning. Thus it is necessary to find ways in which actions such as those set out in Table 1.2 influence what happens in the classroom. As Whiteside (1996:39) reports,

> many [subject leaders] were able to agree that they had met external requirements relating to DfE and Ofsted documentation but few felt they exerted considerable influence on the general teaching of the curriculum area for which they had direct responsibility.

We would therefore wish to highlight the need for subject leaders to look beyond the immediate, and essential, tasks that involve them in the organization of resources, the production of policies, schemes and plans, and the processes for monitoring and evaluation to those tasks that will influence what actually happens in the classroom. This will involve working alongside colleagues in some way, discussing and sharing teaching approaches, recognizing examples of good practice and achievement. We will return to these issues in subsequent chapters and try to show how the responsibilities, roles and tasks of the subject leader can be undertaken in such a way as to have a greater impact on children's learning.

Task 1.3

What do you do as a subject leader that has a direct impact on children's learning? What evidence have you to support your claims?

Subject leader as learner and teacher

It is very appropriate that a school should be thought of as a learning organization. This idea has been developed by other authors such as Southworth (1994:53) who suggested that a learning school had five interrelated characteristics:

- the focus is on the pupils and their learning;
- individual teachers are encouraged to be continuing learners themselves;
- teachers (and sometimes others) who constitute the 'staff' are encouraged to collaborate by learning with and from one another;
- the school as an organisation is a 'learning system';
- the headteacher is the leading learner.

As part of such an organization subject leaders must recognize themselves as learners. No one can be expected to know and understand everything there is to be a subject leader, let alone do it all. Thus steps should be taken to cater for personal and professional development and we would recommend that every subject leader carries out their own personal review, preferably with the head teacher, and prepares a programme which identifies needs, opportunities and provision for learning. Figure 1.2 follows the learning pattern discussed in Chapter 8 and sets out a learning cycle for subject leaders as learners. Schools are also teaching organizations that provide appropriate opportunities for learning to take place. Subject leaders, as we outline in Chapter 8, are teachers of teachers, who are at different stages of their careers, have different levels of confidence in particular subject areas and respond differently to new experiences and the challenges that result as part of the change process.

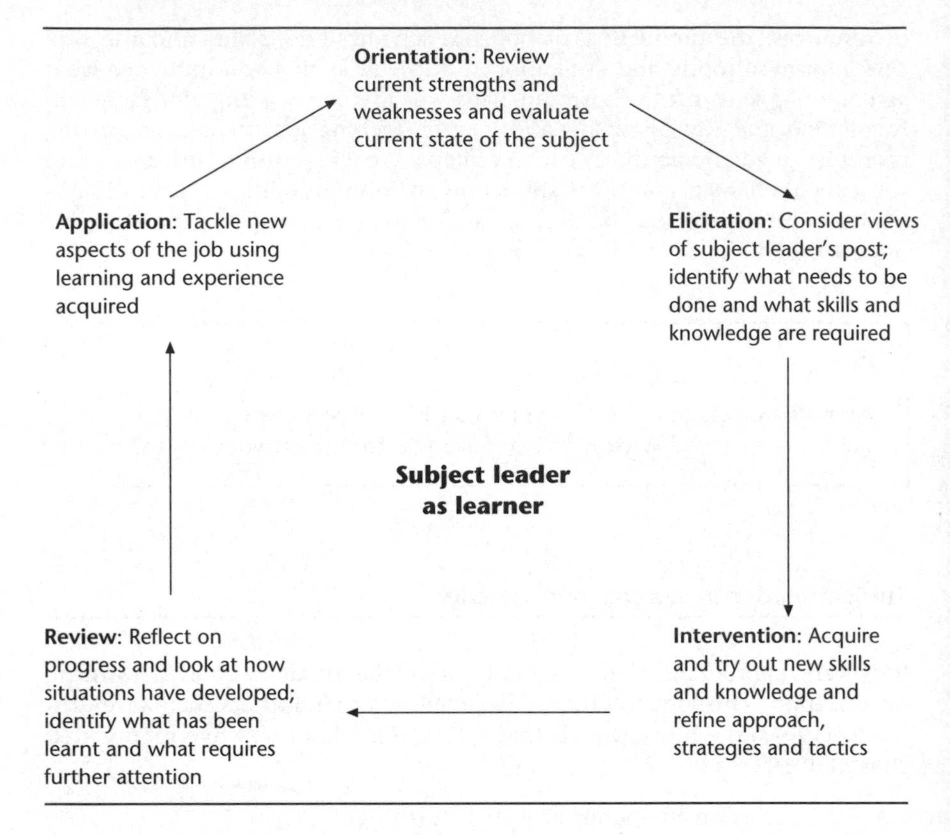

Figure 1.2 The subject leader as learner

> **Task 1.4**
>
> Look back at Table 1.2 and the analysis you did for Task 1.2. Which aspects of subject leadership do you feel you need to learn more about?

Summary

There is no question that the job of subject leader in primary schools is demanding and complex, but it is not impossible. Such posts have a long history but the demands since the early 1990s have raised the profile of subject leaders who are now key figures in developing excellence in schools. By adopting the term subject leader we present the holder as being dynamic and proactive rather than someone which simply reacts to events. To meet the challenges of their responsibilities subject leaders need to show leadership and develop their knowledge, skills and understanding of how they can:

- improve teaching and learning;
- work more effectively with colleagues and others;
- make the most of resources;
- manage change through monitoring and evaluating the impact of the policies, plans and actions that have been put in place.

2

DEVELOPING A LEADERSHIP ROLE

Introduction

Given the changes that schools have experienced since 1989 it is probably not unreasonable to feel that teachers have done well to survive. The fact is that many schools have gone beyond survival. Not only have teachers maintained the good education they previously provided but they have moved forward and improved the quality of experience of the children. School improvement and increased effectiveness have not come about by chance, rather such changes have resulted from the development of:

- professional high quality leadership and management;
- a concentration on teaching and [pupil] learning;
- a learning organisation, i.e. a school with staff who are willing to be learners and to participate in a staff development programme.

(MacGilchrist *et al.* 1997:6)

Clearly the development of a climate in which such characteristics can flourish is heavily dependent on the head teacher (e.g. Fullan and Hargreaves 1992; Hopkins *et al.* 1994; Southworth 1995) who is often seen as the leader with responsibility for setting the overall aims of the school and its management. Everyone in a school, however, has a contribution to make in establishing each of the core characteristics. In particular it is the responsibility of subject leaders to work with their head teachers and their colleagues to bring about the necessary changes that lead to greater effectiveness in their subject areas as part of the whole school development. Leadership, therefore, is not simply the responsibility of the head teacher. There are many situations in which others are required to show the necessary qualities of leadership, for example a teacher arranging a visit from a theatre group. While such examples may appear to be of minor significance, what is important is that someone identified an opportunity, recognized what needed to be done and did it. Subject leaders clearly have a responsibility to provide leadership in their subject areas by recognizing the need and opportunities for change and providing the necessary drive to make it happen. In this chapter we consider what this involves by attempting to answer questions such as: What is meant by leadership and management? What influences the style of leadership? What makes a good leader? What opportunities do subject leaders have to demonstrate leadership?

Task 2.1

Make a list of the situations in which you have acted as a leader in the last month or so. What do you think you did to be the leader in these situations?

Leadership and management

Teachers are leaders every day in that they are responsible for leading their class through the work that needs to be undertaken. This involves, among other things: looking ahead to identify the desired outcomes; planning for how this might be achieved; providing the necessary resources; encouraging the children to undertake the tasks involved; providing the necessary support; questioning and challenging their thinking and actions; reviewing and consolidating progress; assessing what has been achieved; evaluating the success of the teaching and deciding on the next course of action. Although these processes take place in the context of the classroom and children's learning, the steps involved reflect many of the characteristics involved in leadership and management of schools and other organizations, subjects and departments and particular projects and tasks. The major difference is that as a subject leader the role involves working with colleagues rather than with children. While the interpersonal relationships, the context and the tasks involved have changed, the underlying principles and characteristics of being a leader have not.

West-Burnham (1996:54) provides a very useful illustration which emphasizes the importance of a leader:

> Imagine a long and complex journey. It is the role of the leaders to secure agreement on the destination, to ensure that the purpose of the journey is kept firmly in mind and provide guidance and support. Managers ensure that all the resources are available in the right place at the right time, to sort out any detours and obstructions and to ensure that timetables are adhered to. Administrators keep track of the fuel consumption, check that appropriate documentation is available and ensure that managers and leaders can do their job. All three functions are essential but without leadership the journey is, literally, pointless.

Table 2.1 Features of leadership, management and administration

Leadership is concerned with:*	Management is concerned with:*	Administration is concerned with:
• personal and interpersonal behaviour • focus on the future • change and development • quality • effectiveness	• orderly structures • maintaining day-to-day functions • ensuring that work gets done • monitoring outcomes • efficiency	• documents and processes • records of events • preparation of schedules, orders etc. • gathering and processing data • supporting managers and leaders so they can get on with their jobs

**Source:* (Whitaker 1993:74)

Whitaker (1993) stressed that both leadership and management are important elements in making things happen and attempted to set out the distinctions between them using descriptive criteria, included in the first two columns of Table 2.1. We have added a third column in an attempt to give a sense of what administration involves. This is a much maligned activity, which is only really noticed when it goes wrong, yet it is the essential third element in ensuring that what is intended actually happens.

Clearly the post of subject leader involves leadership, management and administration. Each element is important but all too often it is the leadership dimension which is not developed. Our research evidence from the records of subject leaders' activity suggests that many do not have the opportunities to show leadership qualities and that many who do are not aware of the differences between being an effective leader (doing the right things) and being an efficient manager (doing things right). They organize resources prepare schemes, write policies and, less frequently, implement monitoring procedures. Evidence of planning for the future is, unfortunately, much less frequent. It is important therefore that the leadership dimension is brought to the fore by subject leaders:

- establishing a vision of where things should be going whether it is for the whole organization or for a small clearly defined project;
- building relationships with and between individuals in the organization and its teams;
- empowering others to make contributions and accept responsibility for their tasks which contribute to the overall enterprise;
- working creatively to make effective decisions and to solve problems in order achieve the agreed goals.

The translation of these features into practice has never been easy so it is worth considering for a moment what is involved in being a leader. Handy (1985) provided a very clear description of the complexity of the leadership role which is still helpful in guiding our thinking. In particular Handy emphasized the way in which the leadership style may change depending on the circumstances and individuals involved. In some situations an autocratic or directive approach may be appropriate, while in others an open or democratic style might be more effective. In practice the style adopted will often be somewhere between the two extremes. Hence Handy (1985) described this as the 'best-fit approach'.

Factors influencing leadership

The three main elements in any leadership situation are: the leader, the group of people involved and the task to be carried out. Each of these elements puts constraints on, and provides opportunities for, the way in which a situation might develop. To consider these in reverse order, the task that is to be carried out can, and should be clearly defined, if progress is to be made. Tasks may be highly structured with a specific life span or they may be open ended and almost infinite. For example the ordering of materials that are required for the next term is a task that is structured and has a fixed deadline. Thus it may be carried out with relatively little consultation and many of the final decisions may well be made by the leader because of budget constraints. In contrast, revision of the policy and schemes of work is almost constant and never-ending not only because improvements can always be made but also because demands of the curriculum are always changing. This task requires more consultation and will be returned to frequently. In this situation decisions are more likely to be group decisions. The effect of tasks on the way in which the leaders act and respond is influenced by the type of task itself, the time required and that available for completion, the degree of complexity, the margins of error that can be tolerated and the overall importance of the task to those involved.

The group of people involved in the situation will have a major influence on the way the task is carried out and the way in which the leader attempts to move towards completion. The strength of the interpersonal relationships is central in any context although it is important to stress it is often the professional dimensions of the interactions which are critical. We all know of situations where the individuals are very good 'mates' but the job does not get done efficiently – too much time is spent on irrelevant social issues. While on the other hand we have probably experienced situations where members of the group do not mix socially but work very well together and complete tasks very effectively and efficiently. It is not simply the existing relationships in a group that influence the way in which individuals react to the leader and the task, but the previous history and experience of the group can have a significant influence on how it functions. For example, in many schools where there has been little change of staff the memories of 'We tried that once and it didn't work' can often prevent progress being made on particular tasks. It has to be remembered that groups will respond differently from individuals to particular problems and the degree of importance given to the task by the group (or at least key individuals in it) can help or hinder progress. Similarly some groups work better if the task is highly structured with set deadlines, steps and stages, while others feel they should be in control and therefore prefer to let the task unfold. Clearly a mismatch between the group's preference and the type of task can in some situations result in frustration. It is the leader who needs to reconcile the situation so that, as Handy (1985) says, the 'best fit' is achieved.

Exactly how leaders achieve the best fit in turn depends not only on their personal qualities, values and view of leadership but also on the interaction between themselves and their groups. Each party needs to have confidence in, and respect for, the other. If confidence and respect are missing on one or both sides, efforts must be made to identify common ground and start the long process of building bridges. No matter how smoothly tasks are going, leaders are always in a stressful situation since it is their responsibility to ensure that things are brought to a successful conclusion, or at least to ensure that satisfactory progress is being made. How well leaders cope with such stress and their ability to cope with uncertainty will affect how they structure the tasks and interact with the groups. One of the most difficult decisions facing all leaders is the extent to which they do things themselves and how much can be delegated. Leadership does not mean that leaders do all the work, but it does mean that they should have the overall picture and are able to find ways to:

- provide direction and put individual contributions into the overall context so that the group recognizes the value of the work and its components;
- build up good working relationships through clear communication between themselves and their groups as well as between individual members of each group;
- encourage and ensure participation by the appropriate members of a group by using the expertise that is available to best effect;
- monitor and evaluate progress, provide feedback on progress and ensure that the agreed goals are achieved.

Task 2.2

Read Case Study 2.1 and suggest what evidence there is that shows Jill acting as a leader. How did she respond to the demands of the group and the task? Do you agree with Jill's decisions?

Leadership characteristics

What makes a good leader is almost impossible to define, except perhaps to say that it is someone who can manage the demands outlined above

Case Study 2.1 Signs of leadership

Jill has been the subject leader for science in a medium-sized primary school on the outskirts of a large town for two years. When she took up the post she was very concerned that the scheme of work had not been reviewed in the light of the changes to the National Curriculum. Although the school staff had not been notified of their inspection, she knew that it would not be long before they would be and so was determined to get the scheme updated as soon as possible. She was aware that some of her colleagues were very frustrated because the previous subject leader, who had now retired, had been meaning to get round to it for over a year.

Jill talked to several of her colleagues about the best way to go about the task and prepared herself a schedule and target date for completion. The first step was to take the old scheme, try to match it up with the new curriculum documents and then to draft a new scheme which she would present to the staff at a designated staff meeting. This she did. Some minor changes were suggested and incorporated into the scheme, which was completed on schedule and everyone felt they had achieved something. On reflection Jill said, 'I doubt if this is the best way to approach curriculum planning but there are other factors which I must take into account. There is no scheme of work for maths in school since the previous coordinator kept all the notes as we met and discussed it as a staff and on his departure took the only copy. The whole process is now being repeated for maths and the English coordinator is also trying to produce a policy. Staff morale is low so I felt it best to take some of the pressure off everyone.'

Now that they have something in place, Jill feels she can now build on this success and plans to involve her colleagues much more when they tackle the difficult issues of progression and continuity across the KS1/KS2 transition and try to develop a process for monitoring the work in science.

consistently and in a range of situations. Although no one set of criteria can be given, it is possible to suggest that good leaders tend to:

- be knowledgeable about their area of responsibility and about alternative approaches to managing different situations;
- have the ambition, self-confidence and determination to be successful, not simply in general terms but to succeed in the job in which they are currently engaged, showing energy, enthusiasm and efficiency in achieving set goals;
- face tasks with optimism, setting high standards but with a recognition of what is achievable and realistic, when necessary showing a degree of flexibility and the ability to know, differentiate and prioritize what is important, essential, and urgent;

- have good interpersonal skills and communicate effectively and persuasively with others, being willing to give and receive constructive feedback;
- be willing to take responsibility and, when necessary, question authority.

The leadership process

We have stressed throughout the book that leadership is a proactive process and that as subject leader it is important to recognize how the points outlined in the first two sections of this chapter relate to the particular context in which they are being carried out. The next section endeavours to provide examples to illustrate opportunities for leadership. Although we refer to several examples that reflect situations that all subject leaders face at different times, each one can be analysed in terms of a series of common stages that form the type of a leadership cycle which we feel is appropriate to subject leaders in primary schools. Alternative versions of such cycles can be found elsewhere (e.g. Young 1997) but, whatever the words used, they all include elements that involve identification, planning, implementation and review of the tasks involved. Many of the models described, however, do not emphasize the fact that each turn of the cycle should lead into the next. In other words the process, like learning, is more of a spiral than a circle. Thus undertaking leadership tasks involves drawing on the evidence of the past to inform the present which in turn looks forward to the future. We therefore suggest that subject leaders need to be able to:

- anticipate tasks that need doing;
- predict the possible outcomes of each task;
- evaluate evidence relevant to that task;
- consider options that arise from the evidence;
- decide which is the most appropriate action to take;
- act on the decisions in order to achieve the desired outcomes;
- reflect on the outcomes and identify further tasks that are required in order to continue the development process towards more effective teaching and learning.

The culture and leadership style developed by the head teacher provides the overall environment in which subject leaders have to operate. Therefore it is necessary to recognize the strengths and weaknesses of the situation and use them to best advantage. Leadership and management are not always about working with members of a team that is being led nor with those who report to the leader. It is also about leading the senior managers so that they will support the ideas and approaches proposed – we refer to this as the concept of 'leading and managing upwards'. In other words the vision that subject leaders have for their areas of responsibility may have to be 'sold' to the head teacher. It is an important part of leadership to be able to convince those to whom subject leaders are responsible that their ideas and approaches are appropriate and should be supported.

Although we have so far concentrated on the leaders and the roles they play, it is important to recognize that an essential element in the leadership process is the bringing of people together and team building in order to achieve a set of shared goals. Whitaker (1993:75) sums the idea up very clearly when he says,

> leadership is seen as a process which recognises the futility of separating people from each other which seeks constantly to find new and effective ways of integrating human activity, releasing skills and abilities and empowering everyone to a full and active leadership role.

One of the biggest advantages of this type of approach is its potential flexibility so that responses to new pressures can be made quickly, teams can be brought together to complete the task and disband, ready to form a new team to meet the next challenge. For many primary schools this would seem to be an appropriate mode of operation. Everyone is a team leader in some contexts, but in others they are team members and therefore make their contribution in another manner. For example, if a new scheme of work needs to be developed for geography, then the staff, or a subgroup, would come together as a team led by the subject leader for geography in order to complete the task. Yet at the same time an audit of resources for physical education (PE) may be required, in which case a team led by the subject leader for PE is brought together in order to complete this task. Clearly there will be overlap in terms of team membership, but providing everyone is aware of their role in the team and the purpose of the task is clear then the risk of conflict is minimized.

Unfortunately reality is not as clear-cut as we have just suggested, and therefore it is necessary for subject leaders to have an overview of their areas of responsibility in order to make sure that all the necessary day to day things (the maintenance tasks) are done while being alert to opportunities for development and improvement. West (1995) describes what he calls a 'mixed economy' in which the designation of responsibilities for subject areas ensures that the maintenance tasks are undertaken and that task focused teams are brought together to deal with the particular initiatives (the developmental tasks). This is a helpful distinction to which we return in Chapters 3 and 13.

Opportunities to show leadership

Clearly the opportunities for subject leaders to show effective leadership are many and varied. Throughout this book we provide examples, via the case studies, of ways in which different subject leaders have put their leadership skills into practice in areas such as strategic planning (see Case Study 2.3), teaching and learning (Case Study 4.1), professional development of colleagues (Case Studies 8.1 and 8.2), and resources (Case Study 10.1). Key to the success in each situation is the ability of subject leaders to relate to their colleagues and to have a clear view – the vision – of what they would like to achieve.

Case Study 2.2 Developing an approach to leadership

Ann is subject leader for English and special educational needs coordinator (SENCO) in her school, which has recently been formed following the amalgamation of an infant and junior school into a primary with a nursery class. The teachers are of mixed ages and have a wide variety of experience, with many never having taught in a primary school before. Ann is one of the younger members of staff. Although Ann had been a subject leader for some years, this was a new experience and she felt things would take time to settle down as everyone was having to adapt to the new situation, some more reluctantly than others.

In developing her new post, Ann felt that her first priority was to build up her relationships with her colleagues both old and new. In doing so she found that her two areas complemented each other extremely well, sometimes allowing her to kill two birds with one stone. Although she wanted to produce a new English policy for the school, Ann decided not to rush it but spent time trying to support her colleagues, often approaching them to ask if there was anything they needed help with and 'found that people are quite open about problems with children who have special needs and this has proved to be a useful way to gain their confidence'.

Ann then tackled the new English policy by establishing a working party and allowed time for everyone to make a contribution, which she felt was a vital part of trying to get everyone working as a team. She was not unaware of other issues as she said, 'As well as concentrating on the form of the policy I also had to keep everyone focused on the task in order to meet the deadline. Also, I had to consider needs and levels of awareness of the individuals in the group. Dealing with these factors proved just as important as subject knowledge and the ability to write policies.'

One of the most difficult challenges for those who are in a position of leadership is the approach they are going to adopt. As we indicated above this may involve a range of actual styles depending on the situation. Underlying this, however, is the need for subject leaders to develop what could be described as their own leadership subculture. Although the overall school culture will have a strong influence on subject leadership, it is extremely rare for all aspects of the curriculum to be led to equal effect. Case Study 2.2 shows how one subject leader based her approach on building up strong relationships by using a number of strategies.

The importance of recognizing the potential of a situation is essential in bringing about change through effective leadership. Case Study 2.3 illustrates how, upon taking up her post for religious education (RE), a subject leader recognized that there was an opportunity to do more than simply

Case Study 2.3 Taking a strategic view

Chris is the religious education (RE) subject leader in a large primary school in a major city. When she took up the post there had not been a subject leader for several years but the launch of the LEA's new RE syllabus provided a stimulus, partly from the governors, to raise the profile of RE in the school. Chris, who was coming to the end of her first year of teaching, volunteered to take the job on.

Following discussions with the head she agreed that they needed a more consistent approach to RE across the school and that there was a strong case for including much of the personal and social education (PSE) programme within it. Thus she had the start of her vision for RE in the school. Although she did not carry out a formal audit, Chris talked with her colleagues to develop a picture of what was happening in the school. This she found heartening because there were already examples of good practice. The work going on in the nursery and reception classes particularly impressed her. Thus she felt that she could build on what her colleagues were already doing.

Chris felt that it was possible to develop a RE/PSE programme which permeated the life of the school through addressing particular issues and making specific links with other areas of the curriculum. She therefore set a number of targets including:

- short term – set up a working group to prepare a whole school policy and draft scheme of work for RE; get it agreed by the whole staff;
- medium term – identify and establish cross-curricular links;
- longer term – review RE/PSE programme and policy.

write a policy. She had a clear idea of the potential of using RE as a vehicle for developing a programme for personal and social development (PSE) in the school and set about working towards this as fully as possible. Not only did she have the vision for the development, but she was able to share it with her head teacher, colleagues and governors, all of whom were very supportive. Thus having sold the idea it was possible to set short, medium and long term targets aimed at turning the vision into reality.

Task 2.3

Consider your approach to leadership and compare it, in terms of the leadership qualities, styles and processes to that shown by the subject leaders in Case Studies 2.2 and 2.3. Identify the opportunities you have to show leadership and suggest how you might respond to them in order to achieve your goals.

Summary

Effective leadership is not easy and it will never be perfect, but what we have tried to do in this chapter is to set out some principles that will help in improving this role of a subject leader. In particular we would emphasize the importance of:

- providing clear direction;
- building up good working relationships through clear communication;
- encouraging and ensuring participation by the appropriate members of the group;
- monitoring and evaluating progress.

3

STRATEGIC DIRECTION AND DEVELOPMENT

Introduction

Successful and effective leadership, in any organization, depends on how visions, professional relationships, empowerment and creativity are built into an overall strategic plan that provides not only the direction and goals but also the means to achieve those goals. Schools are no different. They are communities in which the success of the leaders is dependent on the way they operate within that community. Thus subject leaders need to be able to translate their aspirations into reality through an understanding of the ways in which this can be done. In this chapter we therefore aim to start this process by introducing the major elements that contribute to sound strategic development. First, we emphasize the importance of establishing professional relationships with colleagues, children, parents, governors and the local community. Second, we set out the value of subject leaders having a vision of where they would like their subjects to be in the future; in particular, what will the teaching of the subject look like if pupils' learning is to be improved? Third, we consider ways in which subject leaders can find out 'where the school is' through auditing the current situation in terms of their subjects. Finally, we stress the importance of establishing direction through development and action planning in the long, medium and short term.

Relationships with others

We explore the development of professional relationships subject leaders need to form in Chapters 7, 8 and 9. At this stage we are simply establishing the importance of such relationships in terms of strategic direction and development of the subject. To this end we highlight the relationships between subject leaders and their head teachers, their colleagues and the children. As we noted in Chapter 2, it is usually the head teacher who plays the key role in creating a vision of the school's overall future direction and this will often be articulated in a school vision or mission statement. It is therefore vital that subject leaders establish good professional relationships with their head teachers (Stow 1989). Ideally, this will be a mutually supportive relationship – subject leaders contributing to the achievement of head teachers' visions and head teachers providing adequate moral, managerial and financial support for subject leaders to meet their responsibilities.

Task 3.1

Identify the strengths and weaknesses of your professional relationship with your head teacher in terms of your subject leader responsibilities. Consider ways in which the relationship could be improved.

Subject leaders need to work at establishing two forms of professional relationship with their colleagues: one in which their colleagues are acting as subject leaders themselves and one with their colleagues as class teachers. Although given less attention in the literature, relationships between colleagues as subject leaders are of particular significance in the context of a subject-based national curriculum, with ever-increasing pressure on teachers to focus on literacy and numeracy. In small schools, where colleagues may have responsibility for several subjects, there is, perhaps, greater potential for ensuring progression and continuity across subjects. In large schools, regular meetings between subject leaders to address issues related to the whole curriculum such as cross-curricular themes and dimensions, approaches to assessment, recording and reporting, school projects/themes, relationships between core and foundation subjects, schemes of work are desirable, if not essential. Subject leaders in related areas, such as science and design and technology, have even greater reason for working closely together – the situation recently observed in a school where these two subject leaders separately ordered their own supplies of batteries and were overprotective about how they were used does not seem efficient.

The manner in which subject leaders relate to their colleagues as class teachers in the context of the subject is potentially going to have the greatest impact on the quality of pupil learning. Sound professional relationships are needed if subject leaders are to create a climate that is conducive to development of their subjects along lines that are congruent with their visions. Achieving this climate will require subject leaders to ensure that colleagues have a clear and shared understanding of the nature of their subject, its importance and role in contributing to pupils' spiritual, cultural, mental and physical development, and in preparing them for the opportunities, responsibilities and experiences of adult life (TTA 1998a).

Task 3.2

Draw a line and place your initials at one end. Consider your colleagues as class teachers and write their initials along the line – with the distance from you indicating the quality of the professional relationship in the context of working in your subject area. Place colleagues with whom you work closely and effectively nearest to your initials. Think about the reasons for your decisions. What insights can you gain from reflecting on these relationships?

The way in which a subject leader relates to the children in a school may not, at first sight, seem to be of significance to the role. However, we would argue that to be successful any subject leader should, as we emphasize in Chapter 4, provide a good role model for colleagues as a teacher of the subject. This is, of course, dependent on the establishment of good teacher – pupil relationships. Additionally, if subject leaders are to foster positive attitudes amongst children to their subjects they need to build sound relationships with children from all age groups and classes. These will aid their attempts to monitor progress in the subject (which may, for example, involve talking to pupils about their work; see Chapter 12) and, when opportunities allow, increase the likelihood that in-class support for less confident colleagues (see Chapter 8) will be successful.

Task 3.3

When do you have the opportunity to relate to children from other classes in terms of your subject? Do you make the most of these occasions as a subject leader? Could these opportunities be increased?

Developing a strategic view

The development of a strategic view depends on subject leaders having visions for their subjects that are shared, and, ideally, owned by their colleagues. Such a vision:

- provides a sense of higher purpose beyond the routine;
- inspires and redirects change;
- encourages ambition;
- fosters commitment to the long term;
- creates consistency of purpose towards improvement;
- anchors decisions;
- helps prioritise developments.

(Avon LEA 1995)

A vision should reflect subject leaders' values concerning their subjects, which, of course, should be values subject leaders encourage their colleagues and school communities to share. Crucially, as well, subject leaders' visions and development planning that results from them should be consistent with the school's overall direction.

Task 3.4

Outline briefly your vision for your subject – where do you want your school to be in five years' time in terms of the subject?

As well as creating positive attitudes amongst staff and establishing a shared understanding of the importance of a subject and a shared vision of the future, the elements of establishing the strategic direction and development for a subject include (based on the TTA standards 1998a):

- developing and implementing policies and practices;
- making use of evidence to inform action;
- establishing, with colleagues, long, medium and short term plans;
- monitoring progress and using analysis to inform future improvement.

The development of policies and practices will be explored in Chapter 5. The other areas are considered in the rest of this chapter. The processes involved in school improvement, within the strategic direction set, are essentially cyclical – the analysis of evidence, gathered through monitoring, informs action plans, which are monitored as they are implemented and this leads to new action plans.

Approaches to auditing, monitoring and evaluation

Why do it?

Auditing is about taking a snapshot to establish where we are at a particular point in time. Monitoring, as an ongoing process, is concerned with improving pupils' learning by collecting information, over a period of time, which will inform the judgements that are made as part of the evaluation. The overall process is aimed at raising standards of pupils' achievement and contributing to external and internal accountability, as well as informing planning. Thus subject leaders are seeking to answer the questions, 'How well are we doing?', 'Are we doing what we say we are – is the school's policy being implemented in practice?' and 'What should we be doing next?'

The answers enable them to evaluate progress towards their visions for their subjects being fulfilled and to decide if targets, set through previous action planning, have been reached. Additionally, of course, Ofsted inspectors (see Chapter 12) expect subject leaders to have evidence gained from monitoring their subjects.

As well as being formative processes, contributing to the development of a subject, auditing and monitoring should be overt and supportive (Waters 1996). Colleagues should know what is going on and why; they should be encouraged to be actively involved in monitoring and value it as a process that contributes to their own professional development. Monitoring of a subject is a responsibility that is often shared between the subject leader and head teacher (especially in small schools). In some schools, governors may also have an explicit part to play. The particular aspects of monitoring that are the responsibilities of the subject leader should be clarified in a job description. Effective and comprehensive monitoring is far easier when a subject leader has non-contact curriculum management time but research evidence (Ritchie 1997a) indicates that many subject leaders do not always have these opportunities. However, it is possible to monitor aspects of teaching and learning without non-contact time. It is important that the approach used is realistic and is appropriate to the development of the subject to date. Good curriculum monitoring, therefore, normally begins with an audit and review of practice – where are we now? – that should highlight strengths as well as weaknesses.

What can you monitor/audit?

There are many different aspects of a subject about which subject leaders can collect data:

- learning outcomes (SATs, test data, children's work);
- learning experiences;
- teaching styles;
- teacher expertise and experience;
- curriculum;
- resources;
- budget;
- professional development needs and provision;
- documentation;
- parental involvement;
- governors' involvement.

For the more experienced subject leader, or head teacher, another aspect of the school, which impacts on the development of a subject and could therefore be seen as an appropriate focus, is school culture and/or management structures (Whiteside 1996). These are discussed in Chapter 13.

Task 3.5

Which of the above do you need to know more about to build up an accurate picture of the state of your subject in the school?

Collecting information

Before setting out on an initial audit, or deciding on the best approach to ongoing monitoring, there are a number of questions which subject leaders should ask themselves.

What will I look at, what is the focus, what do I want to find out about? For example, if the focus is on colleagues' approach to the subject, this might include finding out about their attitudes towards the subject, the subject knowledge (they have or lack), their confidence to teach the subject, their pedagogical skills, the use they make of resources, the nature of their planning etc. It is important for new subject leaders to find out what has been done previously in terms of audits to avoid duplication and to build on existing internal school review processes.

Who will use the information? The audience (e.g. the subject leader, head teacher, whole staff, governors, LEA advisors or Ofsted inspectors) will clearly have implications for the way that colleagues respond to requests and the ownership they feel of the outcomes. In the first instance, an internal rather than external audience may be desirable, in order to encourage frank responses to your requests for information.

What should I expect to find and what are the criteria I can use to analyse the information? For example, if the focus is on a particular aspect of the pupils' learning experiences, such as 'using and applying in mathematics' (Ma1), the indicators of quality experiences in this area could be clarified in advance of collecting the data. There are plenty of sources of such indicators (e.g. Ofsted 1995a) if help is required.

What are the time scales involved? An initial, focused audit may be carried out over a short period, such as a week. Monitoring over a longer period, such as a term or year, is likely for a more experienced subject leader who has been in the school for some years.

How will I collect and record information? It is desirable to involve your colleagues (and head teacher) actively in all aspects of auditing/monitoring, but especially in the collection of information. Strategies for collecting information (examples of some of these in action will be found throughout this book) include:

- observation in classrooms – by subject leader, by head teacher, by other colleagues;
- talking to colleagues (including classroom assistants) – informally, setting up individual interviews, during staff meetings (perhaps, regular meetings

to review progress), at subject leaders' meetings, as part of INSET days, during collaborative classroom work;
- eliciting colleagues' perspectives in other ways – use of self-monitoring, questionnaires, evaluation sheets, logs or diaries;
- talking to pupils;
- sampling / moderation of pupils' work, including examples shared during assemblies, or shown to subject leaders by pupils whose teachers have identified the work as having particular strengths, or showing progress;
- test / SAT results, other published data and pupil records;
- Ofsted and other external perspectives (LEA advisers, higher education institution tutors, students, supply teachers, governors, parents);
- school documentation (school development plans, policies, schemes of work, teacher plans and records);
- physical environment and resources (displays, work areas, storage systems).

Once information has been collected, the data need to be analysed to decide what is significant and can provide evidence to inform future plans, provide insights into achievements or areas of concern. The following questions need answering:

- What have I found out?
- What are the issues that emerge?
- How do I report my findings?

It is important that the limitations of the audit and/or report are acknowledged. It is also valuable evaluating the way in which the audit/monitoring was carried out. What has been learnt to inform the way it might be done next time?

Case Study 3.1 provides an example of how one subject leader used an audit effectively in order to encourage better use of design and technology resources. She also identified two other issues – planning and provision for children in Y5 and Y6 – that needed further consideration.

A relatively new challenge for subject leaders is the need for them to be able to compare their schools with other schools. Subject leaders are increasingly expected to analyse and interpret national and local data concerning pupils' achievements and compare them with their own schools. This is particularly necessary for subject leaders of core subjects, where SAT results, and data related to value-added issues are becoming increasingly complex. LEAs often provide support in this area, but any training is likely to be targeted at head teachers rather than subject leaders. Additionally, subject leaders are expected (for example, by Ofsted) to be aware of general inspection findings and relevant research in the subject (especially research supporting the policymakers' favoured approach, at any particular time, one might add cynically). We will return to monitoring in Chapter 12, where subject leaders' responsibilities during Ofsted inspections will also be examined.

Case Study 3.1 Auditing

Alison is a design and technology subject leader who was appointed to her urban primary school at the beginning of the last school year. She has been teaching for three years. She realized through informal conversations with colleagues that there was a considerable variety of construction kits available in the school, but the use being made of these resources was variable, especially in Key Stage 2. She decided to audit exactly what was available and how it was being used. She produced a simple pro forma that invited colleagues to list what they had and give examples of how they were currently using what they had.

Based on the responses, she identified several issues: some classes had the same kits, but not enough to be useful; there was no continuity through the school; there were some examples of good collaboration in one year group (exchanging kits at different times of the year), but not in others; there was insufficient challenge for pupils at the top end of Key Stage 2; use of construction kits was rarely planned systematically by teachers.

Alison developed an action plan. She negotiated with the head teacher the opportunity to take two staff meetings. At the first one she asked everyone to bring examples of the kits they had to a meeting. She presented what she had found through the audit, introduced her ideas about progression and continuity in the use of construction kits (see DATA 1996) and invited colleagues to consider a more rational means of allocating existing kits around classes and to identify kits that could be shared amongst more than one class. At the second meeting, staff explored ways of including the use of construction kits into their regular planning. They also identified gaps in their current range of kits and helped Alison formulate a case for asking for some money from the PTA to buy some more technical kits for Key Stage 2.

Task 3.6

What data do you receive to allow you to compare your school with others? How could you increase the amount of information you receive? Does your school have a way of measuring value-added aspects of pupils' achievements? How could you show or measure progress from say Y1 to Y3?

Action planning for the future

As we saw in Case Study 3.1, analysis of the information should support decisions about what action needs to be taken, by whom and when. There are several ways to approach this action planning. The findings could be presented to colleagues who can be invited to consider possible priorities. It may help to use SWOT analysis (Whiteside 1996) which involves identifying the Strengths, Weaknesses, Opportunities and Threats of particular developments that have been identified as priorities. This will help in deciding ways forward which might build on current strengths, exploit the opportunities available and minimize the threats involved.

When analysing priorities, it may be helpful to consider the nature of the action involved. As we identified in Chapter 2, some actions involve what could be called maintenance tasks, which need to be done regularly, are relatively straightforward and allow subject leaders to be successful and achieve something. Other tasks will be developmental and are likely to involve much more careful planning, take much longer to achieve and be less easy to tick off. Any prioritizing and action planning by a subject leader should be done in the context of whole school planning. However, the way in which school development plans (SDP) are produced varies from school to school and from LEA to LEA. In some schools these plans are rhetorical or singular (MacGilchrist *et al.* 1995), lacking shared ownership altogether, or owned and used by the head teacher alone. In such situations, it can be difficult for subject leaders to make their planning congruent with whole school planning. In other schools the plans will be cooperative (involving partial ownership) or corporate (involving all the staff in the school, with responsibility shared for outcomes) and subject leaders' planning will be more naturally an integral part of an established process (to which we return in Chapter 5). Whole school planning of developments is increasingly necessary in a climate when national initiatives and directives continue to bombard schools. As we will explore in more detail in Chapter 13, schools (and subject leaders) often have the challenge of dealing with multiple changes.

Another consideration when planning for the future as a result of an audit, or as part of an ongoing monitoring and evaluation process, is the need to consider long, medium and short term targets. In this context, long term is taken to involve three to five years and is usually referred to as 'development planning', medium term between three and 12 months and short term, the next few weeks. It is timely here to remind ourselves of a subject leader's core purpose – improving the quality of pupils' learning. This purpose should inform all stages of development and action planning.

Long term targets should clearly be linked to the subject leader's vision for the subject and the school's vision or mission statement. Ideally, they should be set first, so that the medium and short term goals are focused on achieving the long term aims. Pragmatically, it is sometimes easier to identify and respond to a more immediate need. It is challenging to budget for long term planning, but this is increasingly happening in schools and is preferable to the ad hoc allocation of finances, on a short term basis, still found in some. An essential part of good action planning involves thinking about how the success (of the plan) will be recognized. Figure 3.1 provides a pro forma that may be useful to aid action planning.

Action Planner

Name: ______________________________ *Date:* ______________

What is your concern? What do you want to improve?

What specific aspect of the concern do you want to address?

What ideas do you have about how to improve the situation?

What are realistic goals?

What precise action are you going to take?

Who do you hope will support you? What kind of support do you need?

What evidence will you collect to show you have been able to improve the situation?

When and how will you evaluate progress?

Figure 3.1 An action planner

Task 3.7

Use the pro forma to plan for some aspect of the development of your subject, based on information you have collected during an audit, or recent monitoring.

1 Describe a problem you face, or that you anticipate facing related to your role as a subject leader by:

(a) describing the present situation;

(b) describing the situation as you would like it to be.

2 It is likely that there are some forces pushing in the direction you wish to go and some resisting. Make a list of both kinds:

Resisting forces *Driving forces*

3 Consider these forces and underline those that seem most important. Asterisk those you can influence usefully.

For each resisting force underlined and asterisked, brainstorm as many action steps as you can. Which might you be able to plan and carry out to reduce the effect of the force or to eliminate it?

Resisting force 1 ____________________
Possible actions ____________________
Resisting force 2 ____________________
Possible actions ____________________

Do the same for key driving forces and actions that could increase their effect.

Driving force 1 ____________________
Possible actions ____________________
Driving force 2 ____________________
Possible actions ____________________

Select actions you could realistically take, considering resources available. Plan your action using the following headings:

Action steps *When* *How*

Figure 3.2 Problem solving through force field analysis

When planning for the future, it can help things to go more smoothly if, as we emphasized in Chapter 2, potential problems associated with particular initiatives can be anticipated. A strategy that some subject leaders find useful is the use of force field analysis (which can also be used for other aspects of problem solving). Figure 3.2 provides a framework to support such an analysis.

Task 3.8

Use Figure 3.2 to analyse a specific problem you are currently facing. If possible do this in collaboration with another subject leader or senior manager in your school.

Summary

The development from coordinator to subject leader involves the post-holder taking more responsibility for the strategic direction and development of the subject. This chapter has emphasized the importance of relationships with colleagues and others in the fulfilment of the leadership role, the importance of monitoring the subject, with the aim of enabling development and action planning to meet set targets. The reader should now have insights into the way in which a subject leader can gather evidence to provide an accurate picture of where the school is in terms of the subject. In particular, the need for subject leaders new to the job, or those looking to take their responsibilities more seriously, to carry out an audit of the current situation has been emphasized. The way in which ongoing monitoring can be organized will be revisited in Chapter 12. It is on the basis of this evidence, not impressions, that subject leaders' planning for the future of the subject takes place in the context of whole school planning.

Part II

TEACHING AND LEARNING

4

IMPROVING TEACHING AND LEARNING

Introduction

Teaching and learning should be at the heart of every school and it is a responsibility of every subject leader to help their colleagues provide the best possible learning opportunities for the children in their school at any given time. This can be achieved by subject leaders working at two levels:

- that of the whole school through such activities as the production of policies, schemes of work and resource provision;
- that of individual classrooms through providing a role model for ways in which the subject might be addressed but more importantly by working with colleagues to explore ways of improving the interactions between teachers and children, inside and outside of the classroom.

Alexander *et al.* (1992), among others, have drawn attention to the fact that since the late 1980s there has been a significant improvement in the former but, for several reasons, the impact at the level of the classroom has been more restricted. Southworth (1996) reiterates these findings but goes on to argue that, while the school level of activity is essential, greater emphasis now needs to be placed on what happens at the level of the classroom.

In reflecting on the roles of subject leaders we discussed in Chapter 1, it is not difficult to realize that, in order be successful, subject leaders are required to develop a wide range of knowledge, understanding and skills. The *National Standards for Subject Leaders* (TTA 1998a) outline these in detail. Broadly they are:

- knowledge and understanding of: curriculum development as a process; the concepts and skills in the subject beyond what is required by the National Curriculum; how children learn; the strengths and weaknesses

of different teaching approaches and how they may be implemented effectively;
- the ability and knowledge to: build professional relationships with a wide range of individuals and groups (interpersonal skills); provide effective leadership and management across the whole school; communicate effectively using a variety of media; manage time and resources efficiently; recognize and allow for differences in organizational culture; plan for and implement change.

It is only by combining these elements effectively that further improvements in the quality of learning and increases in standards in primary schools will be achieved.

Defining the curriculum

Debates about what constitutes a curriculum are not new and it is beyond the scope of the present book to provide an in-depth discussion of the arguments for and against various types of curricula, their history and development. It is helpful, however, for subject leaders to be able to put the areas of the curriculum for which they are responsible into a wider context. For example, there has long been a tension between those who view the curriculum as a vehicle for transferring knowledge (or content) and those who argue that the curriculum is about the processes of learning (process). These tensions still exist but, given the nature of the statutory National Curriculum, they often arise in the context of individual subjects. Subject leaders in many subjects have to ensure there is a balance between the content demands and the process requirements of the programmes of study. Subject leaders for science, for example, need to ensure that the processes (of scientific enquiry) are integrated with the content (knowledge and understanding of living things, materials and physical processes) and resist colleagues' inclinations to teach the latter separately.

Kerr (1968:16) defined the curriculum as 'all the learning which is planned and guided by the school, whether it is carried on in groups or individually, inside or outside the school'. Others (e.g. Pollard and Tann 1987) have referred to terms such as the *hidden* curriculum in order to highlight the fact that children do not learn simply from what is planned nor do they appear to learn from everything that is planned. Furthermore it cannot be taken for granted that what is planned is actually what is taught so the *intended (planned)* curriculum is not the same as the *actual* curriculum offered to, and experienced by, the children. An important element of the subject leader's work, therefore, is to try to ensure that what is planned to be taught is appropriate for the children and to close the gap between the *intended* curriculum and the *actual* curriculum as experienced by each individual child.

It is without question part of the subject leader's responsibility to ensure that the National Curriculum, which can be described as the *official* curriculum, is taught to all children as required by the legislation. It is, however, an understatement to say that the introduction of the National Curriculum has had its difficulties (see for example Graham 1993; Coulby and Ward 1996). Each change in the curriculum itself and the associated assessment requirements has put pressure on subject leaders to adjust, among other things, their plans and schemes of work as well as to ensure that their colleagues were kept up to date. Adjustments to the National Curriculum will continue, thus requiring subject leaders to review their interpretation and translation of it into practice.

While it might be argued that the National Curriculum, and initiatives such as those on literacy and numeracy, have removed many of the grounds for debate about the nature of the primary curriculum, we do not feel that this is the case. There is, in fact, a greater need to understand the aims and purposes of the primary curriculum in general and subject curricula in particular. Meeting the learning needs of children is a constant challenge to teachers in all phases of education. The precise demands placed on individual teachers will depend on their particular situation. In the current climate of accountability and Ofsted inspections, however, the major challenge for many teachers is the need 'to be able to readily articulate their teaching – to explain why they are utilising particular approaches, materials, types of classroom organisation etc. and how these relate to the needs of their pupils' (Porter 1996:262).

Meeting the challenge of the curriculum

One of the biggest challenges to improvements in classroom practice is the sheer complexity of the task faced by the class teacher. Unfortunately, the pressures for increased accountability through documentation etc. have taken the emphasis away from the quality of what is actually happening in the classroom. In contrast, the more recent shifts in emphasis by Ofsted and others have meant that greater attention in the future will have to be given to the process of teaching itself. If subject leaders, therefore, are to influence this then they must find ways of working more closely with colleagues in their classrooms. We discuss some of the approaches that might be used in Chapters 7, 8 and 9 but argue here that there is a need for a deeper understanding of the curriculum and teaching itself. O'Neill (1996:220), however, points out that,

> Moving towards an informed overview of the curriculum which is rooted in classroom practice is indeed a significant and potentially very threatening undertaking. It is one which rejects the notion of [subject leaders] providing necessary but basically anodyne arm's-length support for colleagues by merely digesting documentation on their behalf and organising a suitable repository for shared resources.

Subject leaders must open up dialogue as to the nature of the curriculum that is being made available to the children and how the teaching of each subject can be improved. An important starting point is to establish a shared language and understanding of meaning across the different subjects and to establish a degree of consistency in using the terms with colleagues and with children. What, for example, are the similarities and differences in the interpretation of evidence in history as opposed to say science?

One danger is that because the post is that of *subject* leader each subject becomes seen as a discrete entity, in the way much of the teaching is at secondary level, and the wholeness of the primary curriculum becomes lost. If this happens then many of the benefits of primary education as we know it will be lost. O'Neill (1996:221) goes further when he says,

> The likelihood of arriving at a close understanding of the difficulties of teaching and learning essential concepts in, say, music, or art or PE is remote if the dialogue is limited simply to a discussion of the content of the National Curriculum documentation or the formal language often adopted in school based policy documents.

The curriculum is more than the individual subjects and everyone should be working towards a coherence of the curriculum, which provides a continuity of experience based on teaching and learning opportunities across, as well as within, subjects. A policy for learning (see Chapter 5) would support this approach.

Effective curriculum change requires teachers with inside knowledge of the children, the locality, the school culture and environment, to work together in teams to translate the demands of the *official* curriculum in such a way as to meet the needs of the children in their school. It is only in this way that universal issues such as the compulsory curriculum and assessment requirements, models of learning and teaching, equal opportunities, and special educational needs can be addressed in a meaningful manner. Although the curriculum content can be defined, the process of learning is influenced by several other factors (Day *et al.* 1993) as set out in Figure 4.1. Teaching is also influenced by the same factors and it is important for subject leaders to understand how these might influence what takes place in the classroom. It is part of subject leaders' responsibilities to help class teachers understand how these issues relate to the teaching of the subject for which they are responsible.

Influencing teaching and learning

Subject leaders are perceived more and more as having particular subject expertise in that they are seen to possess knowledge and understanding of the structures, principles, processes and content of particular subjects. This has problems associated with it, not least the pressure it can place on an individual subject leader in respect of the level of knowledge and understanding that should be expected. Although there is a continuing debate as

Prior learning
Age, stage and conceptual level of pupil's thinking; have these been effectively diagnosed?

Thinking
Are processess such as interpreting, generalizing, hypothesizing, envisaged? Do you expect practice or transfer?

Sequencing
Does the area have clear delineation and articulation within it? What elements of discovery/guided learning are envisaged?

Differential access
Are individual differences catered for?

Independence/ responsibility
Are these encouraged?

Teaching and learning

Motivation
Are you exploiting known motivation? Can you plan to sustain it?

Self-esteem
Is the work designed to enhance this?

Evaluation
What types are involved? Do they include self-evaluative and diagnostic procedures?

Teacher knowledge/ enthusiasm
Is it an area easily analysed by the teacher? Is it enjoyed? What help is necessary?

Classroom climate/ grouping
What is the optimum form of grouping for this topic? Is interdependence an integrated part?

Figure 4.1 Factors affecting teaching and learning
Source: redrawn from Day *et al.* 1993:91

to the level of subject knowledge required by subject leaders and class teachers, it is generally recognized that an understanding of the key concepts in a subject is a significant factor in effective teaching. Thus it is important for subject leaders to develop their own understanding of their subjects and to help improve that of their colleagues. There are no easy answers but our research suggests that subject leaders are coming to terms with the demands and taking steps to meet the expectations their colleagues have of them. Most importantly they are not setting out to imply that they have all the answers. Rather, good subject leaders are establishing their credibility, not as the fount of all knowledge but as colleagues who are prepared to listen, find out and learn.

In order to help children learn, teachers need to know how to apply their subject knowledge and understanding to the task of teaching, and it is part of subject leaders' responsibilities to support their colleagues in doing this by ensuring that they know:

- how to translate concepts, principles, processes and skills into terms that children can understand;
- how to sequence and organize the skills and content to be taught in such a way as to bring about progression in children's learning;
- what to assess and how to assess it;
- how to diagnose and respond to children's learning needs and difficulties;
- what resources are appropriate and where they can obtained.

The National Standards for Initial Teacher Training (DfEE 1998a) set out the levels of expertise in English, maths, science and information and communications technology (ICT) that should be expected from newly qualified teachers. Standards for advanced teachers, which have also been proposed, will provide further indicators of the level of knowledge and understanding required, as do the self-audit materials also made available by TTA (1998b). Subject leaders will need to use these as guidelines to inform the work they do with their colleagues. By raising issues related to teaching and learning subject leaders will be encouraging, through the types of cooperation we discuss in Chapter 8, the development of their school as a learning environment.

Much can, and has been, done to raise the quality of teaching and learning in the primary school through the improvements in long, medium and short term planning. Evidence (e.g. Kinder and Harland 1991; Alexander *et al.* 1992; Webb and Vulliamy 1995) suggests, however, that unless subject leaders are able to influence the pedagogy of their colleagues, further improvement will be limited. Reasons as to why this area of the subject leader's work has been restricted to date are complex, involving factors such as: the perceptions of the post (Bell 1990, 1992; Edwards 1993); the lack of opportunities for and resistance to subject leaders working alongside their colleagues in their classrooms; the lack of confidence and limited subject knowledge of teachers across the whole curriculum (Webb and Vulliamy 1995; Southworth 1996); and the subject leaders' own level of understanding, not simply of subject knowledge but of the processes of curriculum change and the development of teachers' expertise by different INSET approaches (Galton 1996). The implications for subject leaders are almost endless, but that does not mean things cannot be done. Case Study 4.1, for example shows how one subject leader identified a problem and set up an initiative to address it.

Addressing improvement in teaching and learning

In Chapters 7, 8 and 9 we consider ways of working with colleagues and then discuss ways of managing change in Chapter 13. This short section

Case Study 4.1 Teaching and learning

Kathy, subject leader for geography and ICT in a small school, was concerned that she often saw similar things being done in geography with different years. Although the topics were different, the children seemed to be doing the same things; she felt that there was very little continuity and progression in the teaching that was going on. She therefore decided to try to find out if her impression was correct and put together a questionnaire asking her colleagues to say what they did in geography by detailing the skills, concepts and resources they included in their topics. She summarized the points and persuaded the head teacher to cover her class while she watched some geography lessons in other classes. Following the visits a staff meeting agreed to set up two planning groups, one for KS1 and one for KS2, to look at the findings more carefully.

Kathy meanwhile had taken the opportunity to consult the LEA adviser who had provided her with a framework of skills and geographical concepts linked to the National Curriculum programmes of study. These she discussed with the planning groups in order to match up with the work already going on. The planning groups then came together to look at their findings across the whole school. Kathy agreed to draw up some curriculum maps to show when particular skills and concepts would be introduced so that it was clear how they could achieve progression and continuity throughout the new scheme of work, which was now based on a two year cycle. This had the added advantage that Kathy was able to build in an element revisiting the skills and concepts.

highlights some of the ways in which issues relating to teaching and learning might be addressed at the level of the classroom. First, it is important that subject leaders are recognized as good classroom practitioners, particularly in their area of responsibility. Ideally subject leaders should work towards ensuring that they are seen to be capable of teaching throughout the school and that the work they do is not kept entirely in their own classrooms. Second, in spite of all the difficulties, the idea of working alongside colleagues in their own classrooms can no longer be ignored. Thus subject leaders need to work towards this with their head teachers. The increased emphasis from Ofsted on the quality of teaching provides a very strong stimulus to put appropriate programmes in place. It is essential to acknowledge that conditions make it difficult, in practice, to arrange the necessary cover etc. but it can be done. The key is not to be overambitious in the first instance but to try to put something in place. Those areas of the curriculum that have been selected for particular attention in the school development plan for the year might be the first to benefit, with subject leaders initially being released on one or two occasions only.

Essential to the success of any arrangements, such as those we discuss in Chapter 8, for subject leaders working with colleagues is the need to be very clear as to the purpose of the arrangement, which should be planned and monitored with this in mind. Specific issues need to be discussed on an individual basis but those that are more widely applicable should be raised with other colleagues in order to disseminate good practice throughout the school. Over a period of time consideration might be given to aspects of teaching such as:

- the reasons for and the appropriateness of a particular teaching approach (whole class, group, or individual) and then be extended to such issues as to the quality of the group work. (Are the children working as a group or simply sitting in a group?);
- the suitability of particular activities to achieve the stated aims of the lesson or sequence of lessons;
- the types of pupil–teacher interaction, in particular the nature and quality of the questions being asked;
- approaches to recording by children and display of their work;
- matters relating to differentiation, progression and continuity.

One of the challenges faced by subject leaders is that of encouraging colleagues to discuss and address issues relating to teaching and learning in a way in which it is felt to be relevant to them and their classes. The day to day pressures, for very good reason, often prevent debate at an appropriate level. It is possible however, using some of the approaches suggested in Chapter 8, to tackle many of the key issues via other concerns. For example, discussions relating to:

- the selection and use of resources require decisions ranging from the number of an item needed to the selection of a new published scheme. Each choice is influenced, either implicitly or explicitly, by the preferred teaching approach. Hence it is possible to ask some fundamental questions about why particular choices have been made and what are the implications, if any, for what happens in the classroom. For example a decision to buy enough magnets so that every child can have one to use in a science lesson suggests that the idea of hands on activity is felt to be important. The subject leader might ask whether or not this is the most effective approach and is it something that everyone agrees with. Similarly the selection of a new published scheme requires discussion. Many, if not all, such schemes have an underpinning rationale and the materials are designed with this in mind. Therefore it would be appropriate to ask what this means for teaching the subject. Are any changes required to the way in which teaching is organized? The investment in a new published scheme is diminished if it is not matched by an appropriate teaching approach.
- schemes of work which almost by definition should include consideration of the teaching that will be needed to put them into practice. Unfortunately time pressures sometimes result in the schemes being produced by

the subject leader in isolation and topics etc. are put in place as a result of practical issues and the need to make sure everything has been covered. Very little attention is given to how these will be interpreted in the classroom.

- moderation of children's work and monitoring of their progress quite rightly focus on the children in order to be as fair as possible to them but once again it is an opportunity to ask questions that have a bearing on the teaching process. Is there any evidence that children are interpreting particular activities in a way that was not foreseen? What responses have children made to questions that have been surprising? Looking at questions such as these across the whole school helps to provide a basis for discussions that focus on the teaching and its effectiveness.

Each school has to find its own way of addressing these issues and each subject leader needs to adapt and adjust their mode of working to their own situation. Southworth (1996) helpfully distinguished three groups of activities that can contribute to improvements in teaching and learning:

- activities addressing issues at year group or school level (e.g. joint planning, writing policies, leading staff workshops, mentoring students and new teachers, pairing subject leaders, curriculum reviews, and joint work: visits, concerts, parental events, school assemblies);
- activities drawing attention to the teaching process and classroom interactions (e.g. classroom action research, visiting and observing classrooms, team teaching, explaining and/or demonstrating classroom and teaching practices to colleagues, teacher appraisal, touring the school, and 'showing' assemblies);
- activities focusing on pupils' achievements (e.g. analysis of pupil outcome data, review of pupils' reports, shadowing pupils, monitoring pupils' work, assessment trialing agreements and staff conferences on individual pupils).

We discuss how subject leaders might use such approaches in more detail in Chapter 8.

Task 4.1

Think about the last time you took a lesson in your subject area and consider which aspects went well and which could be improved. List the ways in which you might bring about the improvements, decide which looks the most feasible and try it out. What difference did it make, if any? How might you help a colleague to improve the way they teach the same topic?

Involving parents

In Chapter 7 we discuss relationships with parents as classroom helpers but it is essential to note the importance of parents in children's learning. In this context subject leaders have a responsibility to ensure that as far as possible, parents are kept informed of the overall purpose of what is being attempted in the subject area. Ideally this should go beyond being simply an exercise in communication. Efforts should be made to work with the parents so they know something about the approach that is being adopted, the ways in which their children are being encouraged to learn and the importance of their role as partners in their own children's learning. Once again there are different strategies that have been employed in this area.

For example, in English it is a widely established practice for parents to be involved in the reading scheme for their children, listening to them read at home and talking to them about the stories. The SHIPS project (Solomon 1991, 1992a, 1992b) is an example of how parents might be encouraged to get involved with their children's learning in science. Less formal involvements such as family projects and individual projects on a variety of topics can be used to encourage children to involve their parents in their learning and to build bridges between home and school. Parent evenings during which the subject leader provides a demonstration lesson, with the parents as pupils, are also useful in helping parents come to understand what their child is doing at school and how they might contribute.

Subjects in the curriculum – knowing the subject

We conceived this book to deal with subject leadership in a generic manner because we firmly believe that the overall process and the vast majority of the issues are the same whatever the subject area. Elements of the knowledge and skills required by the subject leader, however, are to a greater or lesser extent subject-specific. Subject leaders should be developing an understanding of what their subject areas involve and those issues that are particularly pertinent to it. Thus in auditing, monitoring and evaluating their subject areas, subject leaders need to identify what is unique about their subject and how the more generic issues are relevant to their subject.

By definition each subject is unique because of the body of knowledge, concepts and philosophy that have been built up as part of the subject over time. It is important that subject leaders develop their own understanding of what might be called the big ideas in their subject, but more specifically those aspects required as part of the National Curriculum and how the subject relates to the rest of the curriculum. Each subject has a contribution to make regardless of its actual status; indeed one of the purposes of the National Curriculum is to provide breadth as well as depth.

In terms of the curriculum, the status of the subject, real or imagined, contributes to its uniqueness. English and maths have always been held in higher regard compared with other subject areas. Therefore even before the formal designation of them as core subjects and, more recently the national strategies for literacy and numeracy, English and maths were given priority in terms of time and emphasis. The importance of science was given a major boost when it became a core subject, but it never has been, and probably never will be, held in the same regard as English and maths. The remaining subjects, designated foundation subjects, provide particular opportunities for children's learning both in terms of their content and the contribution they make to helping children recognize the culture in which they live. Religious education (RE) is required by law but is not part of the National Curriculum. Information and communication technology (ICT) is in a particularly unique position in that it is regarded as being a core element in the curriculum but it should be taught through other subjects. This provides a particularly interesting challenge for ICT subject leaders who need to work with their colleagues at two levels: one to incorporate ICT into the different schemes of work and two, to help develop skills and expertise in ICT for teaching purposes.

All subject leaders need to consider matters such as: teaching and learning approaches; resources; support for colleagues; expertise of colleagues; health and safety matters; and opportunities to develop cross-curricular themes such as health education, moral values and citizenship. Clearly it is not possible to discuss these issues for every individual subject here but subject leaders need to consider in what way the issues apply to their subjects. For example, we are constantly being told that primary teachers lack confidence and knowledge in science so clearly subject leaders for science need to give this some consideration. However this is an issue that applies to other subject areas as well to a greater or lesser extent and so needs to be addressed. Similarly health and safety issues require particular attention in some subjects, for example physical education (PE), design and technology and science, but do not pose the same problems in other subjects. Ofsted reports (e.g. Ofsted 1996a) highlight some specific issues that need to be addressed in the different subject areas of which subject leaders should be aware.

Task 4.2

Make a list of what you consider to be unique about your subject and how the more generic matters, listed in the last paragraph, affect your subject. What implications do the items on your list have for the way in which you carry out your job as a subject leader?

Summary

The key to the success of a primary school ultimately depends on the quality of what happens in the classroom. The development of an appropriate culture and vision for the school, the preparation and writing of policies and plans and the leadership shown by the head teacher are all major factors in bringing about school improvement and ensuring quality, but for the children it is the interaction that they have with their class teacher which counts. Thus in this chapter we have focused on ways in which the subject leader can directly influence these interactions through:

- developing their own understanding of the processes of curriculum change, teaching and learning;
- working with their colleagues both in and out of the classroom; and
- understanding the key aspects of their subject and the contribution it makes to children's learning.

5

POLICIES, SCHEMES AND PLANS

Introduction

The quality of planning in primary schools has improved significantly since the introduction of the National Curriculum (Alexander *et al.* 1992). Most significantly, as Nias *et al.* (1992) noted, the idea of whole school policies and plans is becoming a part of the culture of schools. All primary schools now have school development plans in addition to a range of other policies and curriculum plans. Unfortunately, despite the impact such plans and policies have had in general terms, our evidence suggests there is still work to be done to refine not only the documents themselves but, more importantly, the processes by which they are produced. In this chapter, therefore, we aim to set out how policies, schemes and plans contribute to the overall picture and consider ways in which they can be conceived, developed and implemented effectively.

Defining the terms

One of the biggest difficulties in discussing policies, schemes and plans is the variation in meaning given to, and interpretation of, the terms themselves. The following are used in this book:

- Vision (or mission) statement – this is an overall statement about the aims of the school which tries to encapsulate the ethos and aspirations of everyone who belongs to the community;

- School development plan – this sets out how the school will work towards achieving its aims and identifies the key areas of development for each aspect of the school over the next three to five years;
- Policy – this refers to specific aspects of school life and work, making a clear statement about the aims, objectives, beliefs, approaches, strategies and resources. Policies may refer to specific subject areas or generic issues such as assessment, health and safety;
- Scheme of work – this sets out the main features of the curriculum for the school by term and year and includes details such as the areas of work, the intended learning, and opportunities for assessment to be covered at particular times for each year group. The main purpose of a scheme of work is to ensure that the overall coverage of the curriculum is appropriate, the requirements of the National Curriculum have been met and to ensure the necessary progression, continuity, breadth, balance and differentiation are catered for. The scheme of work thus provides the basis for the long, medium and short term curriculum planning, which helps class teachers sequence and plan individual lessons for their classes.

Deciding which policies, schemes and plans are needed

Figure 5.1 shows how different policies, schemes and plans might relate to each other. Such an overview is helpful in order to clarify the purpose of each element; define the content of each one; show at which level each operates; and indicate who is responsible for the resulting actions required. One of the concerns that arises from research we have undertaken (Bell 1997) is that too many subject leaders work on their policies and schemes of work on their own. In addition to the potential for overlap and duplication of effort, this can lead to subject leaders being isolated in terms of their subjects, not only from their colleagues as class teachers but also from their colleagues as other subject leaders.

Head teachers need to find ways of bringing subject leaders together as subject leaders in order to agree the overall pattern of policies, schemes and plans. Often this does not happen, resulting in a vast number of policies that are not always compatible. It is important, therefore, for the head teacher and subject leaders to take a step back and look at the total package of policies, schemes and plans that the schools needs.

Clearly there are demands placed on schools resulting from Ofsted inspection requirements but there is still room for discretion. For many schools a rationalization of the number and type of policy documents is perhaps overdue, rather than simply adding another one as a knee-jerk reaction to the latest initiative, whatever that might be. This is a clear opportunity for leadership in looking at the whole picture and recognizing the overall purpose of the endeavour rather than simply doing something because it is there. Such a review of existing policies requires some consideration and could save time and effort in the long run.

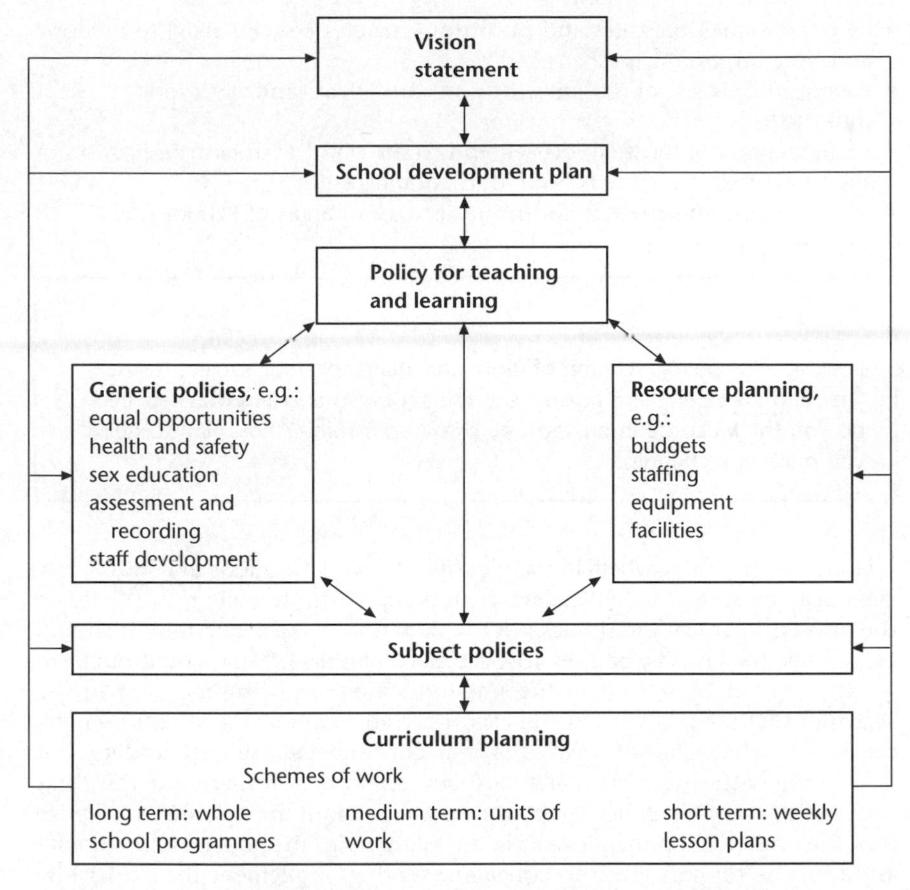

Figure 5.1 Links between different policies, plans and schemes

In evaluating policies, schemes and plans some very simple principles should be considered in order to:

- clarify the purpose of the policy – is it really necessary?
- develop a clear shared understanding of the issues covered by the policy – does everyone know and understand the terms, procedures and processes involved?
- keep duplication to a minimum – is it necessary to include a statement about health and safety in every policy and scheme?
- maximize the value of each task – for example, can the information gathered during an audit be used for more than one purpose?
- identify clear responsibilities for tasks and decisions within the context of the overall pattern – who is going to do what and who has the authority to make the decisions?

- be clear about timescales and priorities – when does this need to be done and how important is it?
- ensure the lines of communication are clear and everyone is kept informed;
- keep documentation well focused and to the point with clear indication of the mechanisms for the actions that should result;
- be consistent and there is continuity across all areas of school life.

Task 5.1

Look at your policy, scheme of work and plans for your subject for next year and consider them against the criteria given above. What aspects do you think can be improved on? Draw up a mini-action plan to help you make the changes.

Gone are the days when it was possible to shut the door and teach 'my class' regardless of what colleagues were doing with 'their classes'. Whatever the pros and cons of the situation a whole school view is required. It should be possible for visitors, be they inspectors or parents of a potential pupil, to see the aspirations set out in the mission statement being manifest in the activities that are going on in the classroom and around the school. Achieving this in their subject areas is a real challenge for subject leaders, but it underlines the need to make sure subject leaders understand the links between the various policies etc. and, perhaps more importantly, recognize how the underlying principles can be translated into the policies and schemes and into the support given to colleagues as they implement them with the children.

A policy for teaching and learning

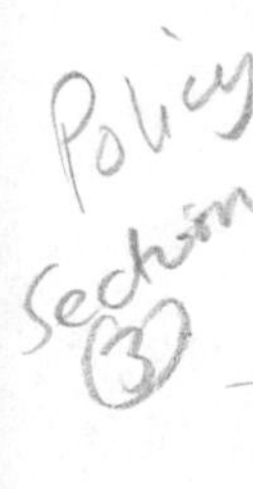

One of the paradoxes in primary schools is the strong defence of a primary philosophy that supports the view of the whole child and the need to look at the curriculum as a whole in the context of the pressures to produce policies etc. for each individual subject without reference to or comparison with others that are produced. This state of affairs can lead to discontinuities and conflict not only for staff but also for the children as they move from one subject to another. West (1995), for example, argues that primary schools should consider developing a generic policy for teaching and learning that is followed in all subject areas. This has several advantages in that it:

- reduces the potential and actual overlap of policies yet at the same time strengthens the core principles;

- provides a sound underpinning for all subject areas thus ensuring continuity and consistency of approach but not producing uniformity;
- highlights the core of the school's activity as a teaching and learning environment;
- makes it essential that the central issues to the profession are debated from time to time as opposed to the day to day matters of implementation.

Such a policy would form the basis for auditing, monitoring and evaluating the teaching and learning across the whole curriculum throughout the school. It should make a clear statement about: what the policy is intended to achieve; what are considered to be the key characteristics of teaching and learning; what is expected of teachers; what are the opportunities and expectations for pupils' learning; and the features of a quality learning environment. Once agreement on such fundamental issues has been reached subject leaders are able to support their colleagues in applying the principles to their particular subject areas.

Why do we need all the documentation?

With many schools in the grip of document overload, an evaluation of policies is all the more important to ensure that the number of documents is kept to a minimum. There is, however, a need for good, high quality documentation that clearly sets out the place of the subject in the school and how the demands for high quality, good practice, school improvement and the requirements of the National Curriculum are to be met. The type of documentation we have in mind would clearly meet the requirements of any inspection process in that it would be comprehensive, coherent, honest and well presented. It should not be produced simply for inspection purposes but rather it should be a working resource that provides direction and support for day to day practice and as such it:

- can provide a clear point of reference and help to remove disputes if verbal agreements have been interpreted in different ways;
- is valuable for introducing new teachers and supply staff to the school's policies and practices;
- helps to provide greater clarity as to the aims of the school because of the discipline and commitment brought about by the need to write things down;
- provides a marker against which progress can be evaluated both locally and nationally;
- can serve as a basis for resourcing, long term planning and evaluating progress;
- provides governors, parents, inspectors etc. with evidence of the school's intentions and something against which to judge the school's practice;

- avoids disintegration of the curriculum organization if the head teacher or subject leader leaves;
- provides continuity until such time as it is replaced.

> **Task 5.2**
>
> Consider the policies, schemes and plans in your school and identify which ones you use and how frequently. Discuss your findings with your colleagues and head teacher. Are there documents that could be thrown away or improved in such a way as to encourage greater use of them? You might combine this task with Task 5.1.

Developing policies, schemes and plans

Essential to the quality and effectiveness of policies, schemes and plans is the manner in which they have been derived. All too often subject leaders write their own and show them to the staff who look at the results and say 'That's fine'. Few colleagues have been involved in the thinking so, while on paper it may seem to be a very good policy or scheme of work, the chances of it being adopted and fully implemented in the way it was intended are very slim. Thus in developing such documents mechanisms have to be used which involve as many staff as possible at appropriate points in a process which will:

- lead to everyone having a clearer picture of the teaching and learning strategies employed throughout the school;
- help to build up teams working towards common, agreed goals;
- develop an appreciation of the extent to which individual actions help or hinder consistency and continuity of the learning process;
- increase the level of commitment and ownership of the decisions and the necessary actions to implement them;
- provide opportunities for different points of view to be expressed and misunderstandings to be resolved at an early stage;
- reinforce the collective responsibility for the implementation of agreed actions and decisions.

Figure 5.2 sets out a possible sequence for the development of a policy or scheme of work that can be adapted for use in most situations. It is important to note the key elements in the process are those required for any such task, that is, a clear definition of the task and its purpose; positive leadership; and the involvement of everyone in such a way as to provide a strong sense of ownership and support for professional development. In addition it is always helpful to remember that ultimately the benefits of the policy or scheme of work are the improvements that should result in

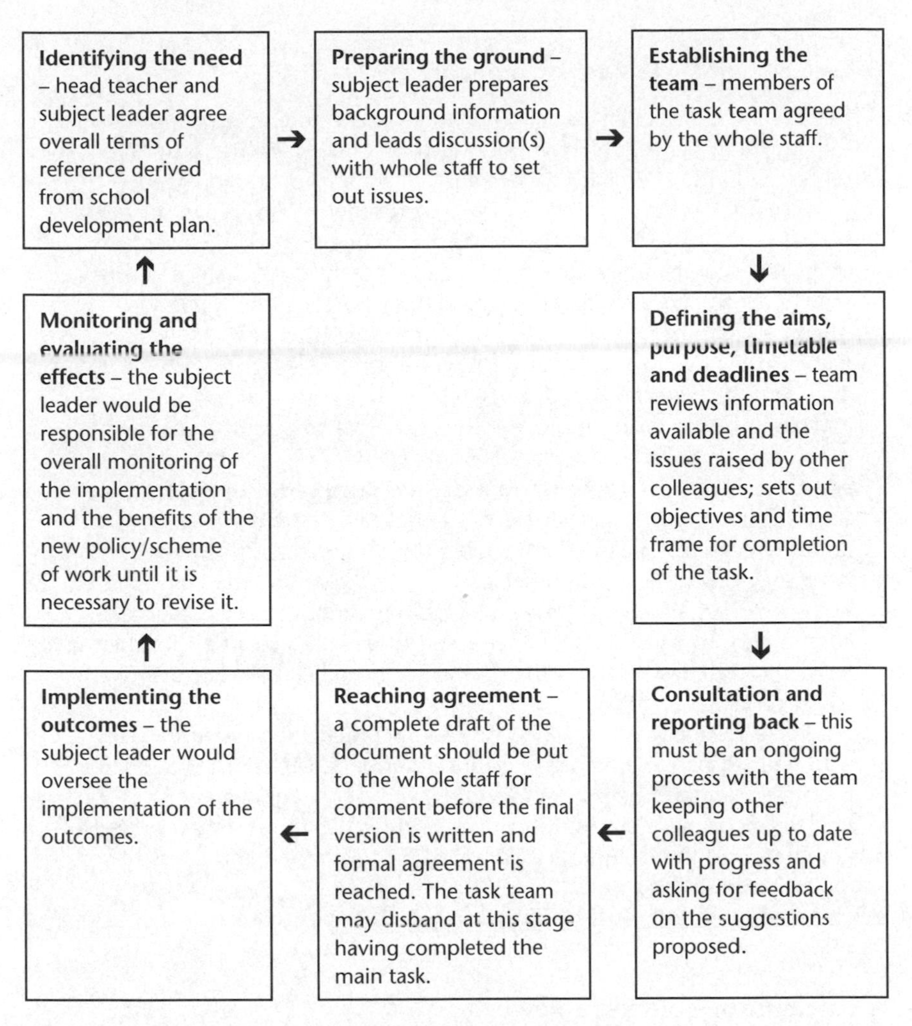

Figure 5.2 Developing policies and schemes of work

learning opportunities for, and achievements of, the children. Case Study 5.1 provides an example of how one subject leader set about developing a policy for English.

Contents of policies, schemes and plans

The exact content of a policy, scheme or plan will depend on such factors as the people involved, the aspect of the curriculum that is being covered, and the stage of development that has been reached by the school. There are, how-ever, elements that one might expect to find in them, which are outlined below.

Case Study 5.1 Developing a policy

Heather, who has been teaching for three years, took over responsibility for English in her school 18 months ago. On taking up her post she recognized, and her head teacher agreed, that a new policy needed to be developed. This was discussed at a staff meeting; everyone agreed that as part of the process they wished to move their practice on and that the documentation should reflect this. Heather used a questionnaire sent to all staff to identify what was current practice and discussed the responses with her colleagues both in groups and as individuals. She was particularly careful to speak to her two 'difficult' colleagues in order to listen to their objections and to try to put their minds at rest.

While this was taking place, Heather was able to attend a course on policy writing and met with the LEA adviser who provided several examples of policies for her to look at. She discussed these informally with the head teacher and some of her colleagues before preparing a draft policy which included an explicit statement about the 'literacy hour' and how it linked to other parts of the English curriculum. This was then used as the basis for a series of meetings to which everyone contributed. In particular, Heather asked them to make sure that they felt comfortable with it and that the aims etc. reflected what they were trying to achieve.

Once agreement was reached on the document, the head teacher, who had supported Heather throughout, arranged for her to do some team teaching and help her colleagues with planning in order to ensure that the policy was put into practice. Heather has found this very helpful in monitoring the changes that are starting to happen and plans to review progress next year.

A curriculum policy framework

A policy document should be a concise statement that maps out the principles on which more detailed curriculum planning, including schemes of work, should be based. Figure 5.3 sets out an appropriate framework around which a policy could be written. It should be noted that if the school has generic policies for sections D, E, F and G the subject policy need only contain those aspects that are specific to the subject (see Chapter 4).

Features of a scheme of work

A scheme of work should always be set in the context of the overall curriculum plan for the school. The scheme will provide an overview of what it is expected every class will cover in any one year. The overall plan also helps to

A *Rationale*

This is a statement that reflects the school's view of the subject/area and its position in the learning process for children.

B *Aims*

These should be restricted to two or three statements about possible long term achievements. It might be helpful to think of the aims as the horizon – we can see it in the distance and we can move towards it but we do not reach it.

C *Objectives*

These should be linked directly to, and derived from, the aims. Objectives are specific and measurable. It should be possible to gather evidence that would demonstrate how well the objectives have been met.

D *Principles of learning and teaching*

This element should outline the principles on which the approaches to learning and teaching are based. Each of the subelements might contain a statement about what is intended and an indication of how it could be achieved:

- **(i)** *equal opportunities, equal access, differentiation and special educational needs;*
- **(ii)** *breadth and balance;*
- **(iii)** *variety of experience;*
- **(iv)** *relevance;*
- **(v)** *continuity and progression;*
- **(vi)** *cross-curricular themes, skills and links;*
- **(vii)** *curriculum design and planning*

Unless there is something unique to this policy, this element could simply refer to overall school framework and planning processes, and the scheme of work for this subject/area.

E *Assessment, recording and reporting*

As with D, this might refer to the overall procedures used within the school.

F *Resources*

This will indicate how the subject/area will be resourced and refer to a more detailed document which identifies the resources that are available and links them to the scheme of work.

G *Safety*

For some subjects, such as science, this will require a specific statement, otherwise refer to the school policy document.

H *Responsibility for this subject/area*

This should state who is responsible for the implementation of the policy and refer to the appropriate job description, for example that of the subject leader.

I *Review*

This states when and how the content, implementation and effectiveness of this policy will be evaluated and reviewed.

J *Associated documents*

This element shows which policies, plans, schemes of work, resource lists etc. this policy relates to.

Figure 5.3 Framework for a subject policy document

Year group	Term one		Term two		Term three	
Reception	Me and my family	Our garden	My house	Toys	Stop, look, and listen	Changing times
PoS						
Published scheme						
Year 1	Living things	Seeds and flowers	Ourselves	Pushes and pulls	Bits and pieces	Sounds
PoS						
Published scheme						
Year 2	Materials	Local habitats	Growing up	Lights	Using materials	Electricity
PoS						
Published scheme						
Year 3	Fruit and vegetables	Properties of materials	Shadows	Making sounds	Making things move	
PoS						
Published scheme						
Year 4	Ponds and streams	Humans and other animals	In the kitchen	Batteries and bulbs	Keeping healthy	
PoS						
Published scheme						
Year 5	Growth of plants	Rocks and soils	Reflections	Changing sounds	Stopping and turning	
PoS						
Published scheme						
Year 6	Woodlands	Solids, liquids and gases	Earth and beyond	Switches and circuits	How the body works	
PoS						
Published scheme						

This plan ensures that all aspects of the National Curriculum programmes of study (PoS) are covered and that concepts are revisited throughout the key stages. The inclusion of a 'free' half term in Y4 to Y6 allows class teachers either to extend an existing topic, introduce an area of interest or to revise work already covered. The rows 'PoS' and 'Published scheme' should be completed to take account of the school situation and provide details of the National Curriculum coverage and the first point of reference for supporting materials respectively.

Figure 5.4 An example of an overall programme for a subject
This example sets out the topic titles for a programme for science but similar programmes should be available for all subject areas (see Ball 1996b:22 for full details)

put each subject and topic into context, indicating what the total planned learning experiences are likely to be for children as they move through the school. Each scheme of work provides the basis of the long and medium term curriculum planning for each subject and from which the detailed short term weekly or daily plans are easily developed for a particular class. Responsibility for the preparation of the scheme of work clearly lies with the subject leader but the individual class teachers draw up their own short term plans.

The long term element of the scheme of work requires decisions to be made as to which aspects of the subject, knowledge, concepts and skills will be taught in which years. This will, of course be strongly guided by the programmes of study set out in the National Curriculum. The context in which the material is to be taught also needs to be agreed on. There are essentially three possibilities:

- a subject-based block of work which relates almost exclusively to the subject in question;
- a subject-focused topic in which the subject provides the major proportion of the content but other subject areas are drawn on to supplement the work;
- an integrated topic in which elements of several subjects provide the material.

The length of time to be spent on this block of work needs to be defined and a check made to ensure that all aspects of the National Curriculum programmes of study are covered. Thus the first part of the scheme of work will provide the kind of information we have set out in Figure 5.4.

The medium term planning element of the scheme of work identifies the ideas, learning objectives, appropriate teaching activities, and learning outcomes for each teaching unit. At this stage attention needs to be given to ensuring that there is a logical sequence in the development of ideas and skill within and between teaching units. It is also valuable to check what is being required of children at the same stage in other subjects in an attempt to build on the skills and knowledge they are acquiring elsewhere. One possible layout for the documentation of each teaching unit is given in Figure 5.5.

It is unlikely that preparation for a scheme of work will start with a blank piece of paper. The existing scheme of work should be available and provide the basis for an audit of what is current practice. In addition to general guidance on planning schemes of work (e.g. SCAA 1995), specific subject exemplars such as the scheme of work for science (QCA 1998a), and detailed support for literacy (DfEE 1998b) and that planned for numeracy are constantly being developed in both paper form and electronically via the Internet. Commercially published materials also include examples of schemes of work. Thus there is a plethora of sources of advice for subject leaders to draw on. Once the decision to revise the scheme of work has been taken it is important to be clear what the issues are and to define clearly what the requirements are for the new scheme. Apart from meeting the specific needs of the school a scheme of work should:

<table>
<tr><td colspan="3">Theme: This sets out the area of the subject covered by this scheme, states the key ideas being addressed and lists the specific aspects of the National Curriculum covered.</td><td colspan="3">Links with other areas of the curriculum: This sets out the specific links with other areas of the curriculum, particularly ICT, numeracy and literacy.</td></tr>
<tr><td colspan="3">Progression: This puts this scheme into context, indicating the work that the children will have covered previously and the work which they will do at a later stage.</td><td colspan="3">Language: This outlines the subject specific language the children have previously encountered and the new vocabulary they will be introduced to.</td></tr>
<tr><td>Learning objectives</td><td>Teaching and learning activities</td><td>Resources</td><td>Learning outcomes</td><td>Points to consider</td><td>Time</td></tr>
<tr><td>These set out the details of the steps that are needed to help learning in this aspect of the curriculum. Points will include:
• skills,
• knowledge,
• ideas/concepts,
• attitudes.
Where appropriate links to the National Curriculum programmes of study should be included.</td><td>The agreed activities that provide the appropriate learning opportunities, linked to the learning objectives should be set out here.
A core of activities might be included alongside alternative suggestions that provide for individual needs and address differentiation.</td><td>This sets out the materials required to ensure that the activities can be carried out effectively.
Particular attention should be drawn to equipment that needs to be specially prepared, booked or is not readily available in school.</td><td>This should indicate the kinds of evidence that show a child has achieved particular objectives. Thus it provides a way in which children's progress can be monitored and evaluated.
Opportunities for particular assessment would be included.</td><td>This provides useful information of points that will improve the teaching of the work covered by the scheme. This might include:
• information about the ideas children might hold in relation to the concepts involved;
• issues about health and safety;
• classroom organization;
• useful 'teaching points'.</td><td>Provides a guide to the time needed to cover the elements of the scheme.</td></tr>
</table>

Figure 5.5 An example of a structure for a scheme of work

Each topic in the overall school plan needs to be set out in some detail and the following provides an appropriate structure.

- cover all aspects of the relevant parts of the programmes of study (PoS) and level descriptions set out in the National Curriculum;
- be a sound basis on which class teachers can plan lessons that meet the needs of particular groups of children and specific individuals where necessary;
- show how the knowledge, concepts and skills of the subject can be built up in an organized, systematic and rigorous manner based on the learning that has already taken place;
- identify lines of progression in the development of skills and concepts through the different topics;
- ensure that the links between the different elements of the subject (e.g. processes such as interpretation of evidence and accepted explanations of phenomena) are explicit;
- link the teaching activities to the learning they aim to promote;
- identify what children are expected to learn and opportunities for assessing children's progress in a way that informs future learning;
- show the links, both actual and potential, with other areas of the curriculum including literacy, numeracy and ICT, and cross-curricular themes such as health education and spiritual and moral development.

Summary

One of the responsibilities facing subject leaders is the translation of the aspirations of their school into practice through the implementation of the curriculum throughout the school. As we discussed in Chapter 4, developing good practice in the classroom is only one of the elements needed to achieve this. It is also necessary to have a map of what it is hoped to achieve and the ways in which this might be done. Thus, as we have outlined in this chapter, there is a need for clearly thought out policies, schemes and plans each of which contributes to a total picture of the school's approach to teaching and learning, which will ultimately have an impact on the curriculum as experienced by the children.

6

EXPECTATIONS AND ASSESSMENT

Introduction

The key factors influencing what children learn are what they already know, what is expected of them and the quality of the interaction they have with their teachers. We would suggest that there is a link between these three factors in that if, for example, we make a judgement that a child is capable of something then we try to match the activities we ask them to do to that expectation. We provide the necessary encouragement to give the child every chance to be successful. In contrast if we consider that another child is unable to do something then we may not even give them the chance to show what they know or can do. It is all too easy to label children, consciously or unconsciously, in such a way as to restrict their access to particular aspects of the curriculum. Clearly this is something we would wish to avoid. Thus in this chapter we will first explore some of the issues relating to expectations of what children can do and achieve and, second, expand the idea of finding out what children know into the whole debate surrounding assessment and the demands they make on the subject leader.

Expectations of what children can do and achieve

'Standards of education in primary schools will not rise until teachers expect more of their pupils, and, in particular, more of able and disadvantaged children' (Alexander *et al.* 1992: para. 107). Clearly this is not an issue that can be dealt with by subject leaders individually; it requires a whole school commitment. Head teachers must take the lead in order to establish the appropriate climate in which it is not only teachers who have high expectations of their pupils but it is also the pupils themselves and their parents. Class teachers will focus on the needs of individual children and schools might wish to consider ways of developing profiling of children (see Ritchie 1991) as a means of reviewing children's progress, exploring their interests and potential and identifying their needs. Thus it is possible to set targets for individual children and, as required for children with special educational needs, prepare individual education plans (IEPs). The process of profiling and its outcomes not only provides valuable evidence about individual children but also provides material to support whole school requirements for assessment and record keeping.

Subject leaders should work towards establishing the specific expectations, standards, targets and other requirements for their subject throughout the school. Establishing appropriate expectations and standards, however, is not easy, as several factors – for example national requirements, the school's position in the league tables, inspection reports, the catchment area of the school – will influence the decisions taken. It is therefore important that any agreed standards are reviewed in the light of experience and increasing evidence as it becomes available. Subject leaders should be aware of the national targets (DfEE 1997), LEA targets for their subject area, and need to draw colleagues' attention to the range of evidence available, including data from external tests, comparisons with similar schools, inspection and research reports and initiatives such as bench-marking of performance of schools. Discussions, based on such information, should lead to the setting of school targets (DfEE 1998c) for pupil achievement, improvements in teaching quality and other parameters, such as attendance, considered to be appropriate.

Expectations do not change unless challenged. It is therefore up to the subject leader to initiate the challenge at the outset of the planning process. As we discussed in Chapter 5, the policies set out the aims for the curriculum area, that is, they are setting expectations encouraging everyone to strive for improvements. The schemes of work include the learning objectives that need to be achieved. If agreement on the aims and objectives is reached through discussion and collaboration then the expectations for teaching and learning are being set. It is the responsibility of subject leaders to ensure colleagues work towards achieving the school targets that have been agreed.

Evidence relating to achievements of children and schools can be analysed in a multitude of ways in order to identify trends and factors which might contribute to a lowering of expectations and perhaps, subsequently, in standards. A variety of social factors such as the number of one-parent families, the number of children on free dinners, and the location of the school all carry implications for what is expected of children in terms of behaviour and achievements. The process of bench-marking in order to make comparisons between schools and within schools has increased in the 1990s, as has the notion of value-added provision. The increased focus on such measurements has made it all the more imperative that subject leaders gather data and use information provided by others, such as their LEA, to evaluate the overall performance of their school in their subjects. We would stress, however, that we do not consider such indicators to be the only criteria against which to measure a school's performance. It is important that subject leaders recognize the significance that might be placed on them by some people, for example governors and parents. It is beyond the scope of this book to discuss all the potential issues related to expectations and targets, but we would wish to highlight two areas for further consideration, first the provision for children with special educational needs and, second, equal opportunities.

Special educational needs (SEN)

Every school should have a special educational needs coordinator (SENCO) who is responsible for children with special educational needs and implementing the SEN Code of Practice (DfE 1994). It is the responsibility of each subject leader, however, to work with the SENCO to ensure that provision for all children is available within their subject area. Subject leaders should try to ensure that the policies and schemes of work include learning opportunities and targets that are suitable for children across the whole ability range.

Children who are high achievers in particular subject areas need to be challenged with activities that not only move their understanding forward but also broaden it and encourage them to apply it to new situations. Class teachers often find providing for such children difficult and look to the subject leader to suggest appropriate ideas. No less of a challenge to both the class teacher and the subject leader is the need to make the subject accessible and to provide suitable activities for children with learning difficulties. One of the major barriers to the learning of such children is the tendency to underestimate their potential. This is supported by evidence from the results of national standard attainment tasks/tests (SATs), which indicate that children with special needs are likely to obtain higher grades on the SATs than on the parallel teacher assessments (Lewis 1995). The implications of this go beyond the formal assessments because, consciously or unconsciously, such expectations are conveyed to the children who respond by working to the levels they perceive are expected of them. 'Crudely, children labelled as slow learners tend to behave that way while children identified as high achievers live up to expectations' (Lewis 1995:183).

Apart from ensuring that appropriate activities are incorporated into schemes of work, subject leaders, in consultation with the SENCO, should endeavour to identify and put into practice the particular strengths the subject has for encouraging children with special educational needs. For example, it is often acknowledged by teachers that children with special educational needs often perform better in science than might be expected. Elsewhere we have discussed the contribution that science can make to the curriculum for children with learning difficulties (see Ritchie 1996; Bell 1998) but, whatever their area of responsibility, subject leaders should encourage:

- the use of a range of teaching approaches that help children with learning difficulties participate through, for example, practical activities, drama, video and ICT, all of which reduce the pressure on pupils to communicate solely through writing;
- strong links with pupils' interests and experience;
- the development of skills, knowledge and understanding in small steps which help to make learning points explicit.

Children with visual, hearing and physical disabilities also require special consideration. The subject leader should be aware of the adaptations to schemes and activities that need to be made to allow access to the curriculum for these children. As with the teaching of children with learning difficulties, the subject leader cannot be expected to know everything but by identifying examples of good practice within the school and sharing these with other colleagues it is possible to build up a repertoire of strategies that will improve the learning opportunities for all children.

Task 6.1

What provision have you made in your scheme of work for children with special educational needs? Carry out an audit of activities that your colleagues have used to support SEN children and set up a discussion to evaluate them.

Equal opportunities

Much has been written about equal opportunities, covering all the possible ways in which individuals or groups of children may be disadvantaged in terms of the learning opportunities that are available them. Every school should have a clear policy and approach to equal opportunities that should be reflected in all aspects of school life. This will refer to, among other things, gender, race, culture, pupils' background and environment, but the important point is that every effort should be made to avoid the temptation to let the stereotypes determine the expectations that teachers might have of individual children and the children have of themselves.

Subject leaders therefore should be aware of ways in which the general statements made in the school policy can be translated into practice through their subject. The monitoring of children's performance in individual subjects throughout the school can be used to identify potential areas of concern and provide evidence of any bias that may be occurring. This monitoring process is essential if issues identified elsewhere (e.g. Ofsted 1996a) are to be addressed. Areas of general concern include: the underachievement of boys, the difficulties encountered by pupils from minority ethnic groups, and the restricted progress of bilingual pupils. In addition, certain subjects have particular issues that must be addressed, such as the position of girls in relation to science and design and technology, and the reluctance of boys to read. It is one thing to be aware of the issues, however, but it is another to do something about it. Thus the subject leader needs to put in place not only appropriate monitoring procedures but also incorporate specific advice into schemes of work, discuss it with colleagues and encourage it to be put into practice in the classroom using appropriate materials.

Assessment, recording and reporting

There is a vast literature dealing with the issues surrounding assessment, recording and reporting and we do not propose to cover the ground again here. Unfortunately the whole area of assessment, record keeping and reporting is part of an emotive debate which has strong political overtones. As Gipps and Stobart (1993:98) claimed, 'the aggregated summative information is there for accountability and political purposes; it is there to evaluate and monitor schools rather than to help directly in the education of individual children'. This situation is a given, as are the demands of accountability imposed by the inspection process. While it might not be ideal, the conditions have increased awareness of assessment and its place in the teaching and learning process. Assessment 'should be an integral part of the educational process' (DES/WO 1988: para. 4) and 'is essential to effective teaching' (Ritchie 1997b:122) as it informs the judgements teachers must make to help children learn.

Although class teachers will carry out assessment of the children in their class, it is for the subject leaders, in consultation with the head teacher and others, to agree upon the overall approach to assessment, recording and reporting and then ensure that this is carried out in practice. Many schools have appointed an assessment coordinator to oversee the process and provide guidance for individual subject leaders. Every subject leader needs to be involved in monitoring, evaluating and reporting on the value and effectiveness, in their subject area, of:

- the planning for and implementation of the ongoing assessment of children's progress in developing the skills, concepts, knowledge and understanding in particular subject areas of the curriculum;
- the range of assessment practices that are used and the development of a coherent approach to and consistent interpretation of assessment outcomes;
- the way assessments are used formatively and diagnostically to inform the immediate, short, medium and long term planning of children's learning;
- the types and quality of feedback given to children;
- the use that is made of summative assessments, records and data that are produced;
- the recording of assessment outcomes in preparation for reporting them to parents, governors and other relevant parties;

- the preparation, organization, arrangements and conditions for those aspects of assessment, including SATs, that are required by law.

Forms of assessment and their use

As class teachers subject leaders will be involved in the day to day assessment of the children in their classes, while as subject leaders they will advise on the type of assessment that is most appropriate for each purpose. Summative assessments should, by their very nature, provide children with the opportunity to demonstrate their skills, knowledge and understanding at a particular point in time, such as at the end of a topic or key stage. Formative assessment will be ongoing and, while assessment activities may have been planned, the main purpose of them is to extend the learning of the pupil. Diagnostic assessment will be much more specific and focus in on a particular aspect of the learning involved.

A wide range of strategies and techniques can be used in assessing children (see for example Novak and Gowin 1984; White and Gunstone 1992; Ollerenshaw and Ritchie 1997) including: tests (both practical and written); the use of drawings, which may be annotated during discussions; cognitive maps including concept maps, floor books; observations of children carrying out a task; and discussions. All these forms of assessment tend to be something that is 'done' to the child but it is important to encourage children to become involved in the assessment process. It is particularly important for children to understand the rules of the game, as it were, so they can start the process of self, and even peer, assessment. Getting the child involved in this way helps them to recognize the key features of their learning. In particular it helps children to begin to identify their strengths and weaknesses and work towards improving their skills, knowledge and understanding. As we suggested earlier the process of profiling and one-to-one reviewing (Ritchie 1991) of children's progress with them has a valuable contribution to make to the assessment process, but more importantly to children's learning. A key task for subject leaders here, particularly at Key Stage 2, is to ensure that the range of assessment strategies are maintained rather than allowing judgements to be made increasingly on tests alone or, as often in the past, relying on informal and impressionistic information (Ofsted 1996a).

Using assessment to inform teaching and learning

A key feature of assessment is the value it has for not only providing information on past progress but also the pointers it provides for future teaching and learning. Depending on the context in which the assessment has taken place, the outcomes of assessment may be used immediately or provide the basis for a much more considered view. Formative assessment is clearly important in helping individual teachers differentiate work in order to meet the needs of individual children, but summative assessments also have a contribution to make, albeit more likely at the class or school level.

It is the subject leader's responsibility to gather together evidence of assessments and try to present an overall picture in relation to pupils' learning and the teaching they receive. The issues we discussed in relation to equal opportunities, for example, are unlikely to be identified unless some degree of analysis is carried out on the outcomes of assessment. Review of intended learning against learning outcomes helps to evaluate how effectively the planned activities are meeting the stated objectives. Adjustments may be required to individual activities or to the scheme in general. For example in science if assessments indicate that overall children are not showing progress in investigative skills then clearly these need to be given greater emphasis in the teaching of it.

Task 6.2

In what ways are the outcomes of assessment used to inform teaching and learning in your subject at the level of the school, class and individual child? How might you make better use of the findings?

Assessment procedures

Every school should have its own procedures for assessment that are clearly set out in the appropriate documents and available to parents and shared with the children. This might involve a combination of standard forms, showing when an assessment was undertaken, the outcomes and the follow up required for each individual child in a subject area. The subject leader may collate the outcomes of such assessments onto a summary chart showing how children are progressing across the school in that particular subject area. The school may have an agreed approach to marking of work and the degree of feedback given to each child. Subject leaders need to work with their colleagues to ensure that marking within a subject area is consistent and gives credit for the work that is being assessed and not simply for 'neat handwriting'. It is clear from inspection reports (see Ofsted 1996a) that there is still room for significant improvements in the marking of children's work. Whatever internal procedures are used, the essential point is that the assessment is consistent, coherent, relevant and manageable.

In addition to the internal procedures, schools are required by law to carry out assessments at the end of each key stage. Currently judgements are made against the level descriptors set out for each subject area and involve several combinations of teacher assessment and external tasks and tests (SATs) depending on the subject and key stage. These requirements at the time of going to press are shown in Table 6.1. Modifications are made to these

Table 6.1 A summary of the requirements for assessment and reporting at Key Stages 1 and 2. The table sets out the minimum requirements the schools must provide for each child

		Key Stage 1		*Key Stage 2*	
Assessment requirements		*R,Y1*	*Y2*	*Y3,4,5*	*Y6*
Teacher assessment	Records of progress	✓	✓	✓	✓
	English		✓		✓
	Maths		✓		✓
	Science		✓		✓
Tasks and tests	Reading		✓		✓
	Writing		✓		✓
	Spelling		✓		✓
	Handwriting				✓
	Mathematics		✓		✓
	Mental Arithmetic				✓
	Science				✓
Reporting requirements					
	Progress in all subjects/activities	✓	✓	✓	✓
	General progress	✓	✓	✓	✓
	Arrangements for discussion	✓	✓	✓	✓
	Attendance record	✓	✓	✓	✓
National Curriculum assessment results	English: teacher assessment overall				✓
	Speaking and listening		✓		✓
	Reading		✓		✓
	Writing		✓		✓
	English: tasks/tests overall				✓
	Reading		✓		✓
	Writing		✓		✓
	Spelling		✓		
	Mathematics: teacher assessment overall		✓		✓
	Mathematics: task/tests overall		✓		✓
	Science: teacher assessment		✓		✓
	Science: task/tests				✓

Source: QCA 1998b and 1998c

requirements from time to time, therefore it is important that subject leaders are up to date with them and communicate this to their colleagues. It is important to remember that teacher assessment is still an essential element of the National Curriculum assessment procedures with the results being reported alongside the task/test results (QCA 1998b, 1998c). Subject leaders need to ensure that the requirements of the National Curriculum assessments are met. This will mean, among other things: ensuring that evidence of each child's ability across the programmes of study is collected together and is available in order to make the necessary judgements; procedures for dealing with papers and other test/task materials are adhered to; and marking is carried out in a professional manner.

Interpreting outcomes of assessment

The value of assessment is significantly diminished if the quality of the information and its interpretation varies from teacher to teacher. Thus in planning assessment it is essential, first, to make sure that the technique is relevant to the stage where the child is and the work they are doing, that is, the assessment is valid. Second, the technique should be applicable to other children in similar situations and is repeatable, that is, the assessment is reliable. The same ideas of validity and reliability also apply to the interpretation of the findings. This places a significant responsibility on subject leaders to ensure that these two conditions are met for the assessments within their subject area. By this we do not mean that they must check every assessment that is done by every one of their colleagues. We do mean, however, that they work closely with other colleagues to reach a common understanding of the purposes of the assessments, the styles and the interpretation of the outcomes.

Much of this can be done through the compilation of a school assessment portfolio of children's work which will:

- develop a consistent interpretation of children's work against the National Curriculum level descriptors;
- provide evidence that the judgements made in the school are consistent and accurate;
- act as a reference point for everyone but in particular newly qualified teachers, new members of staff, supply teachers, governors and, importantly, parents;
- help to reduce the amount of evidence that has to be kept on each individual child.

'The debates generated by agreement trialing and the compilation of school portfolios provide an excellent professional development opportunity focusing on teaching and learning' (Webb and Vulliamy 1996:53). The process of compiling a school assessment portfolio clearly has benefits, but subject leaders are encouraged to make contacts with other schools in order to make comparisons with the interpretations of the assessment requirements that have been made there. In many areas cluster groups already exist, which have facilitated such procedures for agreement trialing either through the LEA or independently.

Recording and reporting assessment findings

The assessment process is closely linked with the need to record and report the findings. Every school has developed its own approach but those in which the process works most effectively have a system that is clear, systematic, consistent and, above all, manageable. Inevitably any recording and reporting system will be a realistic compromise between what is required and what might be desirable. Subject leaders will work towards putting the overall policy into practice for the subject area.

In reviewing the system for recording and reporting, an appropriate starting point is to clarify the purpose of the records and who are they for. To take the latter first, records are required for different purposes by different people so the style of report they receive may well differ. In general terms the records are required by:

- the class teacher, in order to build up a picture of the child as an individual, to identify what has been covered and achieved and to provide an overview of the class performance;
- the subject leader, to be able to monitor overall progress of the children in the particular subject area;
- the 'next teacher', to be able to identify where the child is in any given subject, although unfortunately there is evidence that many teachers do not make effective use of such records when they receive them;
- the head teacher, to get an overview of the standards in the school;
- parents, to see how their child is getting on at school and how they relate to other children;
- governors and inspectors, to identify the quality of education children are receiving in the school.

The types of record needed include first, those that are necessary to meet statutory requirements, which as Ritchie (1997b) notes are 'much more realistic' than they were. These include information on work that each child has covered and their attainment in each subject area. Second, records are needed to build up a picture of the child and an overview of the pupils' performance across the whole school in each subject area. The former is the responsibility of the class teacher and the latter the responsibility of the subject leader, who needs to provide a summary of the information. It is therefore necessary to decide what information needs to be kept for each individual child and what can be kept as a class record. The effort put into careful planning is

Case Study 6.1 Monitoring and recording children's work

This medium sized primary school uses its planning procedures as the basis for monitoring and recording children's progress. The two teachers in each year group meet once a week to review the work they have completed with their class in each of the subject areas and to compare progress with the scheme of work. They annotate changes they have made and note particular difficulties that might have occurred. Agreement is then reached on the work to be covered in the following week. Each teacher then prepares their daily plans for the following week. These plans are available to be looked at by the head teacher and the subject leaders, who are encouraged by the head teacher to visit particular lessons when possible to monitor the work taking place. These visits are usually short (less than 15 minutes) but provide useful insights.

In addition every teacher maintains lesson-by-lesson records. These indicate when the child is present and important points relating to their progress. Significant comments on each child are added to a database, which also contains test results, maintained by the assessment coordinator. Every subject leader can access the database to analyse and evaluate progress in their subject. Thus the annotated planning sheets provide a record of what the class has covered, the lesson registers give information on individual children and the database helps to produce a whole school picture.

rewarded because by annotating the plans for each lesson and unit they can become the record of the work that children have covered. A record sheet for each child can provide evidence of the level of their achievement in National Curriculum terms with brief notes on areas that need further attention. Case Study 6.1 illustrates how one school has attempted to link elements of their planning, monitoring and record keeping.

There is potential for significant areas of duplication in the reporting of assessment outcomes and therefore thought is needed to clarify what is the appropriate type of report for particular situations. Thus class teachers will provide detailed reports on each individual child through the legally required annual report and the more informal report of a child's progress discussed with parents on parents' evening. The annual reports prepared at the end of each key stage are required to include the levels the child has achieved in each attainment target in each subject as determined by the assessment procedures (see Table 6.1). Subject leaders may additionally choose to provide overview reports which outline what has been covered by children throughout the school during the year and the overall levels of performance achieved by each cohort. Such reports will be of interest to governors, LEA advisers, inspectors and contribute to the school profile.

Summary

The main focus of this chapter has been assessment which, in addition to charting the progress and achievements of individual children, makes a significant contribution to teaching and learning. We have emphasized that subject leaders can play a major part in raising the expectations that teachers have of each child and the perceptions that children have of themselves. The following questions, based on Lewis (1996), provide a basis for further reflection on this chapter as well as on the processes for assessment, recording and reporting in school.

- Is assessment sufficiently accurate and focused to inform future teaching and enable the setting of goals?
- Are assessment opportunities built into schemes of work/programmes of learning?
- Do records include details of children's experiences, achievements and, if appropriate, the extent of support provided?
- Is assessment used to monitor progress towards short, medium and long term goals?
- Is assessment used as a way of recognizing and valuing all achievements and progress, however small, in all aspects of the curriculum and in whatever contexts?
- Is children's participation in self-assessment and recording actively promoted?
- What evidence is kept and collated to support teachers' assessments?
- Are the outcomes of assessment reported to the children and their parents clearly?
- Do colleagues make effective use of children's records to inform future development?

Part III

WORKING WITH COLLEAGUES

7 PROFESSIONAL RELATIONSHIPS

Introduction

Effective professional relationships are built on respect and trust and are supported by collaborative school cultures. Having introduced the importance of establishing sound professional relationships in Chapter 3, in this chapter we explore those relationships in more detail and examine ways in which they can be improved. Beyond colleagues in their own school, those with whom subject leaders need to relate include parents, governors, teachers in other schools, LEA advisory staff, Ofsted inspectors, higher education tutors and representatives in the local community, including links with business and industry.

Relationships with the head teacher

The success of particular subjects in school will be affected by the kind of professional relationship subject leaders develop with their head teachers. In some cases the relationships will be unproblematic, with both partners working on the same side, towards shared goals in partnership. In other situations the relationship might need improving. For new subject leaders the nature of that relationship may be influenced by the way in which they were recruited, appointed and inducted into the job. 'Did you jump, or were you pushed?' is an interesting question to ask subject leaders. Research by the authors (Ritchie 1997a) indicates that, in a survey of nearly 100 subject leaders, only 35 per cent applied for the post they held, others were offered it, were asked to take it on, or volunteered. Only 40 per cent were interviewed for the post. Over half were already working in the school, reflected in the fact that only 30 per cent of posts were reported, by this sample, to have been advertised. No matter how the subject leader got the job the appointment process is an opportunity to clarify expectations, responsibilities and roles, and to share values and a vision for the subject. The ad hoc way in which many take on the task means this does not happen very often.

Agreeing a job description is another way of clarifying expectations and it was encouraging to find that nearly 90 per cent of those questioned (Ritchie 1997a) had job descriptions and more than half of these had been negotiated with the post holder. This compares favourably with findings by Bell (1992), which indicated that only a fifth of his sample had job descriptions. This increase can be put down to a number of factors including teacher appraisal and school development planning (Webb and Vulliamy 1996). However, job descriptions are not always well written and can be vague, confuse responsibilities and roles and lack focus in terms of identifying tasks that can be realistically tackled. Evidence, from our ongoing research, indicates that more schools are starting to supplement the job descriptions of their subject leaders with agreed annual targets. The benefits of this approach are only starting to become evident but the views expressed by the subject leaders and head teachers show that agreed annual targets help everyone focus more clearly on what is important for that year, the particular stage of development of the school and the level of expertise of the subject leader; and, as part of the monitoring and evaluation process, assist subject leaders recognize when progress is being made and acknowledge achievements.

Job descriptions should be unique to the individual subject leader and the school concerned and as such will provide a basis for a constructive professional relationship between head teacher and subject leader. Acting as a 'contract', the job description makes it clear what both sides will contribute to ensure the development of the subject within the school. Table 7.1 sets out headings that could be used for a comprehensive job description.

Task 7.1

If you have a job description for your work as a subject leader use the following questions to analyse it and consider ways of improving it.

- Does it avoid vague statements and unnecessary jargon?
- Does it make your responsibilities explicit?
- Does it avoid overprescriptiveness?
- Does it include specific targets/tasks that have to be accomplished in a fixed time scale and distinguish these from more general aspects of the job?
- Does it include references to your personal and professional development?
- Does it ensure there is no duplication of tasks carried out by others in school?
- Does it inform other colleagues of your roles and responsibilities?
- Is it an appropriate document to be used in the context of your appraisal? Was it negotiated and is it reviewed regularly?

Table 7.1 Outline for a job description

Name
Job title
Job purpose
Objectives
Major responsibility areas
Key roles
Key tasks
Responsibilities (related to current SDP)
Support available – non-contact/budget/INSET
Other specific responsibilities
Responsible to
Review date

Source: based on an example from Stoke Lodge Infants School, South Gloucestershire LEA

There are many ways in which head teachers can support subject leaders and, equally, ways in which subject leaders can maximize support. Evidence from subject leaders (Ritchie 1997a) indicates that the majority feel well supported by their head teachers. This support was described most frequently as moral support, or in terms of financial/resource support and non-contact curriculum management time. The ways in which coordinators suggested that head teachers' support could be improved included: more time (most common); additional finance and, in many cases, responsibility for a budget; help in target setting; guidance and practical help with monitoring (a key area where head teacher and subject leader responsibilities often overlap); support in dealing with 'difficult' colleagues. In some cases, frustration was expressed because expectations and responsibilities were not always made clear by head teachers and job descriptions were not always realistic (as also found by West 1996). There was also evidence of some coordinators wanting to do more, if they were given the responsibility and appropriate support.

Stow (1989) described head teachers as tending to fall into one of five categories: non-supportive, nominally supportive, indecisive, dictators (not delegators) and fully supportive. Table 7.2 provides a way of labelling the roles head teachers might play in their relationships with subject leaders.

The way head teachers do their job clearly has a major impact on the school culture and will affect the role of the subject leader as an agent of change (see Chapter 13). Additionally, the way a head teacher views the job of the subject leader will impact on the way a subject leader can fulfil the post's requirements. For example, Osborn and Black (1994) have shown that for heads the key roles for subject leaders are 'distillers' and 'disseminators', whereas Moore (1992a) found heads regarding subject leaders as 'helpers' and 'fellow workers' rather than 'advisers' or 'decision makers'. Subject leaders therefore should be working to develop their relationships with their head

Table 7.2 Relationships with head teachers

Head teachers can be positively seen as:	More negatively they can be:
• inspirers,	• blockers,
• supporters,	• dictators,
• collaborators,	• controllers,
• consultants,	• non-interventionists,
• experts,	• uninterested managers.
• critical friends,	
• advisers,	
• information-givers,	
• negotiators,	
• providers.	

teachers so, for example, in the area of strategic leadership and development, they can influence head teachers' visions for schools so that the subjects they represent are given an appropriate priority in their schools' development. Subject leaders should seek to hold annual review meetings with their head teachers focused on their subjects. These reviews might address the following (adapted from Cross, 1998):

- pupils' achievements;
- action plans, targets and progress to date;
- priorities;
- progress with regard to policy and other documentation;
- any events or activities planned;
- resources, including recent and future purchasing;
- monitoring and evaluation.

Task 7.2

Consider your relationship with your head teacher and, using Table 7.2, identify the roles adopted by the head. List strategies that will help you minimize the negative and maximize the positive aspects of the way the head supports your subject leader work.

Relationships with other colleagues in school

Subject leaders work with a variety of colleagues in a range of contexts. Curiously, there is evidence that subject leaders feel less well supported by their colleagues than by their head teachers (Ritchie 1997a). Yet all subject leaders are in a situation where, as classroom teachers, they also play a role where they could (and should) be supportive of colleagues acting as subject leaders in other subject areas. Why then, one wonders, is this support not forthcoming or not perceived? The answer probably lies in the notion of school culture again – and 'how we do things around here'. In a collaborative culture, support is welcomed and given with equal enthusiasm. Perhaps this is less likely in other school cultures, where vested interests or insecurity dominate. An analysis of the way in which subject leaders perceive their colleagues' support indicates that supportive colleagues were: participators, sharers, collaborators, supporters, enthusiasts, innovators, critical friends. Less supportive colleagues were: resistors, blockers, hoarders, passive receivers.

Task 7.3

Analyse your colleagues' responses to you as a subject leader in terms of the typology given, adding other labels that seem appropriate. List strategies to overcome the difficulties inherent in the less supportive attitudes and maximize the support provided by positive colleagues. Reflect on your own attitude/response to colleagues who are seeking to support you wearing their subject leader hats. How would they categorize you?

A major factor in establishing good relationships with colleagues is their respect for the subject leader generally and in particular as a teacher of the subject. Consequently, establishing credentials as a good practitioner will be an important first step, especially if the subject leader is new to the school. This is a particular challenge for a newly qualified teacher (NQT) or relatively young or inexperienced teacher taking on the job of subject leader. There can be benefits to being prepared to go public about a preferred approach to teaching the subject. Subject leaders might consider: putting up displays outside their classroom; sharing examples at assemblies; inviting colleagues into their room (informally or in a more systematic way); inviting parents to work in their classroom; sending pupils to share examples of their work with the head teacher or other teachers; talking about what they are doing with colleagues and sharing the things that have gone well, but being honest about the aspects that need to be improved. No one expects subject leaders to be 'superteachers', indeed, such a label can be unhelpful. Creating an atmosphere/ethos where the subject is talked about and not ignored or marginalized (particularly if it is a foundation subject) is necessary if subject leaders are to fulfil other aspects of their job. It will also encourage their colleagues to look to them for help if they see the subject leaders making efforts to keep well-informed – going on courses, reading subject journals, going to cluster meetings, inviting subject leaders from other schools to visit etc. Such activities are difficult to fit in alongside the challenge of being a class teacher, but they are important if subject leaders are to be successful.

Case Study 7.1 Subject leaders extending their professional relationships

Jo is the deputy head of a large primary school and is overall subject leader for English. She has the support of two colleagues, one for each key stage, who make up the English team that meets on average once a week. For a variety of reasons, but particularly because it was felt that many of the subject leaders were unsure as to what was expected of them and because the size of the school meant that practice varied considerably, Jo felt there was a need to get together and try to identify some common practice. She therefore called a meeting for subject leaders. This inevitably included nearly all the staff but it was stressed that it was a meeting of subject leaders, not a staff meeting.

The subject leaders produced a list of the things they thought they were expected to do and agreement was reached about what they all should do. They agreed that a group of them would set out and trial a simple matrix to help them plan and set targets for themselves over the next two terms. The matrix, based on the seven functions of subject leaders described by West (1995), included: subject knowledge, advice and documentation, resources management, assessment, communication and public relations, review and evaluation and monitoring quality.

The immediate advantage of this approach was that the subject leaders became much more aware of what each other was doing and it highlighted aspects of the school development plan that were being missed in particular subject areas. Overall it was felt that this approach provided a much more focused way of setting targets for subject leaders, which helped everyone appreciate what was taking place elsewhere in the school.

Relationships with other subject leaders

Whole school planning has fostered relationships at this level but in many schools they are still in their infancy. Therefore it is worth subject leaders exploring areas where such collaboration is desirable: for example, issues of continuity and progression in areas such as 'independent learning', 'collaboration and systematic group work', 'problem solving', 'using investigative skills' etc. It could also be useful for subject leaders to work together on the generic skills and understanding related to their posts. This could involve exploring for example the management of change, or the skills needed as a 'critical friend', in order to help develop a common awareness which will benefit the whole staff. Another area that could benefit from closer collaboration between subject leaders is cross-phase transfer where different schools are involved (or in some cases, improving continuity across phases within the same school). Case Study 7.1 provides an example of subject leaders working together.

In addition to the need to develop relationships with other subject leaders in general, there are some specific links that have to be made. The focus on core skills means that English, mathematics and ICT subject leaders have particular responsibilities for liaising with other subject leaders to ensure that core skills are developed within other subjects. The need for subject leaders to establish and implement policies and practices for assessment, recording and reporting (TTA 1998a) provides the need for collaboration with the school's assessment coordinator.

Subject leaders have a particular responsibility for working with the special educational needs coordinator (SENCO) to ensure that individual education programmes (IEPs) are used to set subject-specific targets, where appropriate. In some schools and subjects this can be a significant part of the work. Subject leaders are likely to be the ones with the best understanding of the National Curriculum requirements and an understanding of how pupils learn in their subject. It is, therefore, appropriate that they contribute to setting realistic targets for individual pupils who are having difficulties. Equally, subject leaders may, in a different context, be the most suitable person to plan or teach a tailored programme of work for high achieving pupils.

Relationships with recently qualified colleagues

Any subject leader will have a mix of colleagues – those with limited experience (as NQTs or returners to the profession, who have had a career break to raise a family) – who will need support. These colleagues will vary in terms of the confidence and competence to teach a particular subject. The approach subject leaders take should be based on their judgement about the needs of each colleague, informed, ideally, by evidence collected through an audit or other systematic needs identification exercise (see Chapter 8).

Recently qualified teachers will have particular needs, especially in their first (induction) year of teaching and subject leaders may be key people in supporting their transition into the profession. The current standards for NQTs (DFEE 1998a) and the nature of the requirements on teacher educators can mean that many new entrants have had limited training in some of the foundation subjects in particular and the expectation is that they will receive support from their first school. The subject leader should be aware of an NQT's needs and negotiate the support required with the head teacher as well as the individual concerned.

New entrants will bring with them a profile of their competences, gained through their training – their Career Entry Profile (TTA 1997). Often they will have been used to a process of action planning to address their professional needs, which can be built on in school and lead into a constructive approach to appraisal when the time comes.

It is also worth remembering that the enthusiasm and professional knowledge NQTs bring with them to their first post may also have potential for supporting the aspirations of a subject leader. The National Standards for

Initial Teacher Training (ITT) (DFEE 1998a) are very demanding, especially in core subjects and ICT. Consequently new entrants to the profession should be well qualified, for example, to share ideas of ways ICT can support learning in particular subject areas. There will also be standards established for the induction year, which should inform subject leaders' decisions about how they support NQTs.

Relationships with student teachers

While considering the nature of initial teacher education, it is worth reflecting on the needs of student teachers who might be in school. Subject leaders have a role in supporting student teachers in their subject. It is common for them to have directed tasks to carry out in schools that are subject specific. Such exercises can provide subject leaders with a means of gathering helpful information about their subject. Thus the best person to negotiate with them about the tasks is clearly the subject leader providing opportunities for a partnership to develop. For example, linked to their science course, student teachers might be expected: to elicit pupils' ideas about a concept at different ages; to examine school approaches to recording assessments of pupils in science investigations; or to discuss short, medium and long term planning in the subject. Most student teachers focus on at least one subject specialism so, as potential subject leaders in a subject, will need particular support and advice, and hopefully, a dose of enthusiasm to motivate them to become effective subject leaders themselves when the opportunity arises.

Relationships with classroom helpers

Classroom assistants and parents as classroom helpers are two other groups that may, at certain times, need support and guidance from a subject leader. An afterschool briefing or workshop for classroom helpers about the subject and the role of adults in children's learning can be a valuable and efficient way of ensuring there is continuity of experience for pupils (it may also offer benefits for your colleagues if they attend). An example could be: in design and technology when the input might focus on the safe use of tools; or in English, related to paired reading strategies.

Working with governors

It is becoming common for individual governors on a school's governing body to take responsibility for specific subjects. Consequently, that individual is one with whom a subject leader should establish a good working relationship. That governor will need to be briefed and supported in understanding the nature of the subject and the approach taken in school. It is worth subject leaders being proactive and inviting 'subject' governors to visit them in their classes. This will help increase governors' awareness of the demands on teachers and the resource/accommodation issues that might later arise in the governing body. In an ideal situation, such governors will be allies and supporters – they may even be enthusiasts for a subject who can offer practical help in school. The informal opportunities to relate to governors can often be more constructive than those offered in the formal context of meetings. When governors are visiting school subject leaders need to ensure they are made aware of what is going on in relation to their subjects: drawing attention to school displays or new resources, getting the children to talk to them about what they have done over the last few weeks, perhaps reminding them of a particularly successful lesson or topic. The National Association of Governors and Managers (NAGM 1994) provides valuable guidance on visiting classrooms.

Subject leaders are often asked to provide a formal presentation to the whole governing body about their subject generally, or specific issues or needs at a particular time. These presentations are important and need to be thoroughly planned. They can be rather threatening, especially if it's the first time the subject leader has been asked to attend a governing body meeting. The issues about planning such inputs have much in common with the way a presentation for colleagues might be planned (which will be dealt with in Chapter 9). Alternatively, subject leaders may have to write a paper outlining developments in their area over the last year, or indicating future developments. Again, effort is needed at the planning stage to ensure the subject is presented in the best light and gain governors' support for the subject leader's vision and what it is hoped to achieve.

Liaising with other professionals

Subject leaders will work with a variety of other professionals in the context of their job. For example, it is desirable to establish good links with teachers (especially their opposite number) in feeder schools and nurseries. This can have unexpected benefits such as gaining new insights into teaching methods and resources linked to particular subjects. It can also lead to raised expectations of what children can do if they are seen in action just before they transfer. It is essential to ensure children experience continuity between phases. The same applies to schools to which children move on. Primary–secondary liaison can be a problematic area and requires a book of its own. However, it is worth the effort to establish good links, especially if it eases the problems so many children face as they move from KS2 to KS3.

In many areas, clusters of schools work together and meetings of specific subject leaders are regularly arranged. Where these happen, subject leaders seem to gain a lot from the opportunity to talk and share concerns with colleagues in a similar position. Playing an active role in such cluster groups can provide enriching professional development for those involved. If such meetings are not happening in their area we would encourage subject leaders to explore the possibilities of setting them up – LEAs are often keen to support such initiatives.

Liaison with LEA advisory staff is another aspect of subject leaders' work. Although advisory teachers are increasingly rare they still exist in some areas for some subjects and provide a valuable source of support for subject leaders. Subject leaders should know what support is available in their LEA and make the most of it. LEA staff are likely to be providing a programme of professional development from which subject leaders can benefit. Relationships with advisers/inspectors may have a different feel from those established with advisory or support teachers. It is likely that contact with advisers/inspectors in school will be in the context of a school review or pre/post-Ofsted inspection. In such situations subject leaders may not be prepared to share their concerns and seek their help but it is worth remembering that it is in the interests of the LEA that its schools do well in inspections. Relationships with Ofsted inspectors are dealt with in Chapter 12.

Tutors from higher education institutions (HEIs) are also members of the education community with whom subject leaders may have professional contact, whether it is related to work with ITT students in school or through professional development activities. HEIs provide a range of accredited courses that may help address some of the needs of subject leaders and their colleagues. For example, it is not uncommon for HEIs to run courses aimed at addressing the needs of subject leaders in terms of individual subjects or the generic aspects of the job. HEI tutors may also be used in a consultancy role, to run INSET days or afterschool sessions (see Chapter 9). It can be hard to be a prophet in your own land and having someone else come in and give a message the subject leader has been giving consistently can lead to more immediate results, especially if such an input is built into a planned programme of support.

Other sources of support for subject leaders are the subject professional associations (see the Appendix). There are many reasons why subject leaders may wish to join associations as individual members, but if that is not possible the school, at least, should join as an institutional member. This helps to ensure subject leaders are kept regularly updated about developments in their subject and the latest thinking on teaching and learning, as well as getting reviews of new books, resources and equipment. Attending annual or regional conferences of subject associations can be excellent professional development as well as a good way of refreshing enthusiasm – meeting others who share the same interests (and challenges).

Making the most of the community

Subject leaders should be looking for opportunities to maximize the help and support that can be provided by the local community. The role of parents as partners in their children's education has already been referred to in Chapter 4. Parents, however, can be a resource for children's learning in a more general way. This may be sharing particular expertise, enthusiasms, interests or experiences (coming into the school to talk about visits to foreign countries; reminiscing about previous times; demonstrating tools and equipment they use at work; talking about having a baby; teaching a craft that they do). There will be others in the community with a less direct link with the school who might be prepared to play a similar role. Many schools already exploit the opportunities that exist for local visitors, visits or the provision of resources. However, there are ways in which subjects might benefit that have not been tried. Some subject leaders have proved very successful in obtaining local sponsorship for events and curriculum activities. One enterprising design and technology subject leader resourced a whole school project on environments by appealing to local companies for recycled materials (see Ritchie 1995a). Links with local businesses can foster enterprise awareness, which is a cross-curriculum dimension that can be developed in most curriculum areas. Subject leaders should be identifying ways in which this dimension can be addressed explicitly and making contacts with those who can support such learning. With older children, mini-enterprise projects can be a motivating vehicle for learning (see Ritchie 1995a). Additional benefits of involving the local community relate to the school's profile. In many areas, especially urban settings, schools are in competition with each other for pupils. This is not necessarily a desirable state of affairs, but it is a reality and the school's profile in the locality can have an effect on recruitment.

Task 7.4

Look at the topics/themes being covered in your subject area over the next two months. With a colleague (if possible), consider the opportunities for involving the local community in ways that would enhance the learning opportunities for pupils.

Summary

Human relationships are complex and depend on the individual personalities of those involved. Professional relationships are a subset of such relationships and are at the heart of successful subject leadership. There are no simple formulas for making these relationships work, although we would argue mutual respect is an essential factor. This chapter has considered the variety of professional relationships that a subject leader needs to establish and develop. Some, such as those with colleagues, are part of the general professional role of teachers, others, such as links with advisory staff, may be more specific to the roles of a subject leader. However, the focus of the chapter has been those aspects of the relationships which are to do with the subject and the improvement of pupils' learning in that subject.

8

SUPPORTING COLLEAGUES ON AN INDIVIDUAL BASIS

Introduction

Professional development involves learning to do something new or to do something better. In Chapter 1, we drew attention to the idea that subject leaders are learners, here we consider the role of subject leaders in supporting their colleagues as learners. Figure 8.1 compares children's and teachers' learning and illustrates this in terms of the phases of what are often called 'constructivist approaches' to learning and teaching: orientation, elicitation, intervention, review, application (Ollerenshaw and Ritchie 1997). This chapter explores these parallels and examines how the subject leader can contribute to the process.

Subject leaders find many opportunities to offer support and advice to their colleagues. Sometimes these opportunities occur informally and the subject leader grabs a chance to share some information or responds to a request for ideas or resources. This might happen at break time, over a cup of coffee, in the classroom or after school. The importance of such encounters cannot be overemphasized. For many subject leaders it is these informal 'conversations with a purpose' that are a key element of their effectiveness. On other occasions the support will be organized more systematically and be offered in a more formal context. This chapter focuses more on the second type and considers strategies for eliciting colleagues' needs, planning to meet those needs and implementing a programme of support that can be evaluated.

The way in which support is offered (and received) will depend on many factors: personal relationships, the subject leader's status and experience, the origins and nature of the particular teacher's needs etc. A fundamental question is whether the support is being offered in what might be called a collaborative mode or in a way that suggests an 'expert' supporting a 'novice'. It will be evident from what we have already said that the subject leader

	CLASSROOM WORK		PROFESSIONAL ACTIVITIES	
	Teacher's strategy	**Children's learning**	**Teachers' learning**	**Subject leader's role**
Orientation	Scene-setting activities/ unstructured exploration	Engaging with context, becoming curious/ stimulated	Reflection on current practice and professional understanding	Introducing colleagues to issues/ideas/ skills related to the subject
Elicitation	Helping children to find out and clarify what they already think and can do	Structuring existing ideas about area of study/ exploring existing skills	Structuring existing values/ ideas about teaching and children's learning and identifying concerns	Helping colleagues identify their professional needs and planning ways of meeting those needs
Intervention	Encouraging children to develop, test out and refine new ideas and skills	Restructuring ideas by extending, developing or replacing them /developing new skills	Trying out new strategies in the classroom (perhaps with support) and evaluating them	Supporting colleagues: collaborative planning and evaluation, workshops, classroom work/coaching
Review	Helping the children to reflect on the learning experience and outcome	Thinking about learning that has taken place and how it resulted	Reviewing progress during 'coaching' phase and review of professional development	Acting as 'critical friend' to help colleagues identify progress and the reasons for it
Application	Providing challenges or contexts in which new ideas and capabilities can be tried	Application of what has been learnt to new situations/ everyday life	Applying new professional competence and understanding to everyday teaching situations	Supporting the application of new teaching competence: whole school development initiatives/ schemes of work

Figure 8.1 Parallels between children's and teachers' learning

should have some expertise in the subject, but it is also our contention that support is best provided in a collaborative way that recognizes both sides have something to offer and something to learn.

The choice of whom a subject leader targets for support and when is another sensitive issue, especially for those new to the job or school. Should support be offered or requested? Should it be optional or compulsory? It is likely that all colleagues will have some professional needs related to a particular subject, although these may not always be recognized and they will certainly vary over time. The head teacher should have a part to play in helping subject leaders make decisions about whom to work with and negotiation with the head is the starting point. However, it may be tempting for a head teacher to identify a member of staff who is a 'problem' that they have not been able to solve. So subject leaders need to make sure they get a chance to share their opinions. We are convinced that it is better to begin with a friend, who will work willingly, rather than banging your head against a brick wall. The best approach may be an open invitation for colleagues to identify themselves for support and then to discuss with the head teacher who to work with from those who have volunteered. Alternatively, the head teacher may have identified specific needs related to the subject through the appraisals that they have done with colleagues. The following sections assume that someone has been identified for support and explore ways of offering that support.

Identifying needs

Providing professional development opportunities for colleagues should involve the explicit identification of their professional needs through the exploration and clarification of their existing practice. This is the structuring or elicitation phase of the constructivist approach illustrated in Figure 8.1. However, colleagues' needs and wants may not be the same, so identifying needs, as others have found previously (Bolam 1982), is not easy. Individuals are not always the best at identifying their own needs – 'they may not know what they don't know'. The relationship between needs and wants is therefore an important starting point. Wilson and Eason (1995) offer the framework in Figure 8.2 for analysing the relationship between them.

Task 8.1

Think of examples of situations where you can recognize your own experience (or that of your colleagues) fitting each of the possibilities in Figure 8.2.

There are other issues to consider with regard to needs identification. One is the potential mismatch between individual, school, local and national

		WANT	
		Do	**Do not**
NEED	**Do**	Ideal (as it suggests an informed analysis of needs)	Very difficult (as it suggests a conflict of deep-rooted beliefs/values/perspectives)
	Do not	Fairly common and may present difficulties (as it suggests a difference of perception about existing practice and possibilities)	Ideal (as it suggests an informed analysis of needs)

Figure 8.2 The relationship between needs and wants
Source: adapted from Wilson and Eason 1995

needs. Another is the power-related issue of who defines the needs. It is likely that some colleagues will have needs related to their future careers that will not necessarily be congruent with school needs. It is also possible that senior managers will have an agenda regarding individuals' needs that is at odds with those colleagues' own views. Subject leaders should be helping colleagues identify needs, clarifying the origin and nature of those needs, and perhaps exploring the extent to which needs and wants are different for a particular colleague. Needs that are also wants, and recognized as such, are much easier to meet – teachers are much more likely to be motivated and eager for support if they consider it is helping them achieve what they want, rather than working towards someone else's goals.

The professional needs of teachers are varied and complex, relating to subject and pedagogical knowledge, skills and understanding as well as an awareness of issues and attitudes. The challenge is to help colleagues articulate needs in a way that is specific enough to enable action to be planned which addresses those needs. When working with colleagues to identify needs it is important to have an open mind and be able to help them explore their needs at a variety of levels, perhaps beginning at a general level and working towards more specific needs. Some colleagues may find any attempt to identify their needs as threatening – exposing 'weakness' is often problematic for teachers and should only be initiated when strategies for meeting those needs can also be offered. Subject leaders may have colleagues who could be described as 'unconscious incompetents' – they are unaware of ways in which they are ineffective or of other approaches they could be taking. However, they may be content. It is too easy to turn them into dissatisfied 'conscious incompetents' who know what they should be doing and know that they are not. Such a step should only be taken if there are the time and resources to help them address their concerns, that is, to help them to become 'conscious competents'. This is an important point for subject leaders as it is essential that they are clear about what can be dealt with and what cannot in the particular circumstances. In other words it is essential not to set unrealistic expectations which lead to colleagues feeling let down.

Strategies for identifying needs can be as varied as the needs themselves. Clearly a dialogue is likely to be involved, but the stimulus for that can be organized in numerous ways. For example: sharing and discussing pupils' work; evaluating a lesson based on the individual teacher's perception of it; evaluating a lesson that the subject leader or someone else observed; staff discussion about particular aspects of the subject; collaborative planning of a topic or unit of work; development or implementation of a scheme of work; visit to another classroom to observe the subject leader or another teacher; watching a video of classroom practice or reading case studies; discussing individual children's achievements and progress; whole school topics or projects. Each of these provides opportunities to explore professional needs. For the dialogue to be successful it is necessary for the subject leader to use a range of interpersonal skills effectively.

One way of conceptualizing needs is to recognize them as aspects of professionals' practice that are not congruent with their educational values. We all hold a set of beliefs or values about learning and teaching that inform the way we work with children. However, the constraints of real classrooms and children often mean these values are 'denied in action' – we are 'living contradictions' (Whitehead 1989). Identifying colleagues' needs is often about helping them recognize when their values are at odds with their practice. In this sense, the needs might be better labelled as concerns. The subject leader can help a colleague explore concerns and focus on a specific aspect by using open-ended questions such as those based on guidance materials from NCET (1989): How do you feel about . . . ? In what way . . . ? What other possibilities were there . . . ? Tell me about . . . You seem to be saying . . . Say a little more about . . . Go on . . . Can you explain that . . . ? What are your thoughts now . . . ? So, are you saying . . . ?

Task 8.2

Work with a colleague with whom you get on well. Organize a 15 minute discussion with them in which you explore a concern that they have about their teaching of 'your' subject. Attempt to use some of the above questions to focus your colleague on a specific aspect of their concern which could be the target of support you provide.

Planning to support colleagues and implementing plans

The first step in planning what action should be taken to address needs is to analyse those needs in terms of what support is appropriate, which aspects of them can be supported by the subject leader and which needs would be better addressed through external support. A subject leader should know what is available locally and nationally. Sometimes a teacher's needs will be best met through a course, perhaps provided by the local education authority (LEA) or a local higher education institution (HEI). There are some excellent distance-learning packages available (such as Open University material) and, increasingly, materials on the Internet that can be used by individuals or teachers working collaboratively.

If the support is going to be provided within school and by the subject leader then a detailed action plan can be developed, ideally through further discussion between those involved. This might involve the following stages:

1 considering new perspectives;
2 setting realistic goals;
3 generating new ways forward;
4 planning precise action;
5 implementing the new approach;
6 evaluating the approach.

This process has parallels with action enquiry or action research approaches (Ritchie 1995b; Ollerenshaw and Ritchie 1997). Subject leaders are thus supporting colleagues as they engage in a cyclical process of plan, act, observe and reflect (see Case Study 8.1). The goal of this process is to enable them to live out their values more fully in their practice. In other words, to enable teachers to do what they say they want to do. It is a tool to help teachers reduce the extent to which they are living contradictions.

Some interesting research carried out into the effectiveness of advisory teachers (Harland 1990) is relevant to the current discussion. Harland proposed a framework to describe the roles adopted in supporting colleagues which can be simplified to give–tell–show–ask. For a subject leader, this might mean giving a colleague something to help them (a new piece of science equipment; a new game for use in mathematics; a collection of artefacts to encourage evaluation in design and technology) or, alternatively, telling them about new ideas for teaching a topic. Harland found both strategies were appreciated by the recipients but there was little evidence some months after this kind of support, offered in isolation, that there was any long term impact on the teacher's practice. A strategy that seemed to lead to greater impact was 'showing' by, for example, taking a colleague's class while they watched. However, again if used as an isolated strategy, it also had quite limited impact on long term changes to a teacher's classroom work.

In Harland's research the strategy that seemed to offer most potential for effecting long term change was one that was least favoured by the recipients and was the one which proved to be the highest risk strategy – sometimes it had a negative result on the professional relationship. This strategy, which Harland called 'zetetic', is a 'let's enquire together' mode, involving the subject leader as a critical friend, helping their colleague as the teacher engages in an enquiry to improve their practice. We consider there to be

Case Study 8.1 Working with colleagues

John is a mathematics subject leader in a large urban primary school. He is given a few hours a week non-contact time to provide in-class support for colleagues. He had been asked by Jill, a Y5 teacher who had taught at the school for 15 years, to help her introduce more mental maths activities. She felt this was an area in which she lacked confidence and experience. She recognized its importance to children's learning in mathematics, but was unsure how to make it work. John spent 20 minutes with her after school one evening discussing what she already did and exploring other approaches she could adopt. She was keen to try more whole class interactive teaching. John outlined some activities he had tried and between them they decided to focus on a number square game that Jill thought would work with her class. They planned a 20 minute teacher-led session followed by 15 minutes of group work, which Jill invited John to observe. They agreed that John would focus on the responses of a group of boys who Jill identified as not having a positive attitude towards mathematics. During the group work, John and Jill had a chance to chat informally about their first impressions of the lesson. They had a more detailed discussion at lunch time. John was able to provide some positive feedback about Jill's teaching and the positive response of most of the class. However, two boys in the focus group that John was observing had lost concentration after the first half of the teacher-led session. This led to further discussion about how they might be more actively involved in mental maths activities and a new cycle began . . .

considerable benefits to this collaborative approach, if it is handled sensitively by the subject leader.

However, the best strategy is probably a combination of those roles outlined and use of the cycle proposed by Joyce and Showers (1980), which recognized professional learning in several stages:

1 presentation of new skills;
2 modelling of new skills;
3 practice in simulated settings;
4 feedback on performance in simulated or real settings;
5 coaching/assistance on the job.

Such a framework has parallels with Figure 8.1 and offers a model to help in planning of support for colleagues. Case Study 8.2 provides an example of these steps in action.

There are clearly numerous approaches that can be adopted to support colleagues and address the needs they have identified. Keeping colleagues up to date with changes or developments in your curriculum area may be most

Case Study 8.2 Planning support for colleagues

Jane is a design and technology subject leader in a rural school of 150 pupils. She was supporting colleagues in introducing new cutting and joining techniques with wood in their classes. She ran a workshop after school and demonstrated the skills involved (1). Colleagues tried out the techniques at their own level, with Jane's support (2). At the end of the session she invited them to reflect and comment on her role as a teacher during the workshop. A few days later, Sally, an older teacher who wanted to improve her design and technology teaching, visited Jane's class for half an hour, while the head took her class for PE. She worked with a small group of children, while Jane worked with the rest on a different activity (3). These children had some experience of using wood, but needed more practice. Sally supported them as they constructed money boxes. At the end of the session Jane and Sally discussed how it had gone and what lessons Sally had learnt which would help her introduce similar work to her younger class (4). A few weeks later, when Sally had worked with several groups in her own class on the techniques, she invited Jane to pop in and see how the work was progressing. Jane was able to provide positive feedback, but also to remind Sally of some of the health and safety points she had made in the original workshop (5).

efficiently managed through written material, especially if time is not available in staff meetings. Written materials can also be useful for other purposes and suit some colleagues' preferred learning styles. For example: a history subject leader produced guidance sheets to accompany a collection of old kitchen implements, showing how they could be used for a series of lessons within a topic on the Victorians; an RE subject leader produced notes on using some of the storybooks in the school library for religious education activities. Simplified, self-produced written guidance concerning the use of new resources can make them far more attractive to colleagues and more likely to be used.

Task 8.3

Identify some aspect of your curriculum area that would benefit from written guidance for colleagues. Produce a sheet and invite colleagues to use it and comment on its usefulness to them.

Another strategy that does not involve support in the classroom is to work with a colleague or colleagues on collaborative planning (perhaps within one year group). This is increasingly common in schools now and has considerable potential for offering support and guidance in an unthreatening manner. Ideally, joint evaluation after plans have been implemented can increase the impact of the support. This provides opportunities to help colleagues review what they have learnt from the experience and what they can do in the future. This form of support involves subject leaders acting as critical friends in the same way as discussed above in the context of supporting colleagues' action enquiries (Case Study 8.1).

Support in the classroom can take several forms, some of which have already been mentioned: demonstration lesson with a whole class; team teaching with a colleague (with each taking a lead role at different points in the lesson); work with groups of children which a colleague can observe as they work with the rest; focused observation of a colleague's class to help identify concerns or plan new ways forward. It is crucial to avoid being used simply as an extra pair of hands. It is important to remind colleagues that the purpose of being in their classrooms is to support them and their learning; the children are the vehicle for this, but the goal is *adult* learning.

For subject leaders, teaching or working with other classes provides benefits which go beyond the support it offers colleagues, by: increasing their experience of, for example, an unfamiliar key stage; helping them to understand more about progression in their subject area; allowing them to trial ideas, materials or strategies that have worked with their class; providing them with evidence to inform discussions with other teachers or the whole staff; and providing them with the opportunity to monitor the work of other classes.

Evaluating support offered to colleagues

Support for colleagues needs to be properly evaluated, especially where non-contact curriculum management time is being used to do it. Providing non-contact time makes a significant call on school budgets and needs to be justified. Subject leaders need to know whether the approaches they are using are having an impact in classrooms – is the quality of children's learning and achievements in the subject area improving? There is also the added benefit of colleagues seeing subject leaders practice what they preach. In other words, if subject leaders are encouraging colleagues to be critical of their own practice and make judgements about the effectiveness of changes to their practice on the basis of evidence not impression, then subject leaders should be doing the same in the context of their subject leader work.

There are various ways of evaluating the work with colleagues, ranging from an informal discussion to more systematic collection of data. Evaluation strategies will be discussed in more detail in the next chapter and these can easily be adapted to evaluate support for one or more colleagues. Clearly, there are links between evaluating such work with colleagues and monitoring. The evidence that is collected from colleagues about the support they have received and its impact on children's learning, is evidence that has other purposes and can help improve the picture showing 'how well we're doing around here' (see Chapters 3 and 12). Additionally, the links between evidence collected by subject leaders and their colleagues' self-evaluations and/or appraisal may be significant.

Earlier in this chapter we recognized that not all the support that colleagues need can be provided from within school. If they are involved in professional development outside, perhaps through an LEA or HEI, it is also important for subject leaders to monitor this when it relates to their subject area and evaluate the impact of it in school. Setting up systems to do this will also alert them to opportunities for disseminating such learning to the rest of the staff. Too often the benefits that individuals obtain from in service work outside school are not shared sufficiently well with others in the school. It is part of subject leaders' work to ensure these benefits are maximized.

Summary

The National Standards for Subject Leaders (TTA 1998a:5) indicates that a key outcome of subject leadership is teachers who

> work well together as a team; support the aims of the subject and understand how they relate to the school's aims; are involved in the formation of policies and plans and apply them consistently in the classroom; are dedicated to improving standards of teaching and learning; have an enthusiasm for the subject which reinforces the motivation of pupils; have high expectations for pupils and set realistic but challenging targets based on a good knowledge of their pupils and the progression of concepts in the subject; make good use of guidance, training and support to enhance their knowledge and understanding of the subject and to develop expertise in their teaching; take account of recent and relevant research and inspection findings; make effective use of subject-specific resources; select appropriate teaching and learning approaches to meet subject-specific learning objectives and the needs of pupils.

This sets a challenging agenda for subject leaders in terms of the way they support colleagues. This chapter has addressed that support and emphasized the importance of systematic needs identification and analysis to inform planning that is focused on meeting those needs. It has also stressed that all support should be evaluated to ensure it is having the impact on pupils' learning that was intended. It has also been clear that the subject leader can gain benefits from the process of supporting colleagues. It is often said that the teacher learns more than the taught – subject leaders can get as much professional learning from providing support as the colleague being supported.

9

WORKING WITH GROUPS

Introduction

This chapter focuses on the work of a subject leader with groups of colleagues in a variety of different contexts, for a range of different purposes. The skills required when working with groups are not always the same as those needed when working one-to-one. Working with groups involves greater emphasis, at times, on the leadership dimension of the post. The subject leader will need to adopt a range of roles in the context of staff meetings, team meetings (perhaps working on specific tasks) and in-service education and training (INSET) days. Additionally, there will be other situations where a subject leader is working with a group, for example governors or parents. The chapter also reinforces the need to see any individual sessions and activities for colleagues in the context of an ongoing process of school improvement. Consequently, we stress the need for appropriate preparation before sessions and follow up afterwards.

Staff meetings

The afterschool staff meeting is the most regular group forum in which the subject leader will be operating. At times the subject leader will be leading these meetings, at others 'representing' the subject's interests. This will involve a variety of roles, such as organizer, presenter, chair, contributor, recorder, listener, mediator and facilitator. Case Study 9.1 illustrates one subject leader's approach to a staff meeting.

Staff meetings with a subject focus in which subject leaders take a key role can take a variety of formats including: a presentation, discussion and summary; structured discussion with the whole staff; discussion in groups with

Case Study 9.1 Leading a staff meeting

Helen is a science subject leader in a small rural primary school with five classes. She was attending an accredited course, provided by her local higher education institution, running over a year. She was invited by her head teacher to use one of the staff meetings each term to disseminate aspects of the course. During the autumn term the staff were focusing on assessment and so Helen decided to introduce some strategies she had met on the course. She hoped this would encourage her colleagues to try them and improve the assessment of their pupils' learning in science. She was beginning to use floor books and concept maps with her Y3/4 class. She collected some examples to share with her colleagues. At the meeting she presented her view of children's learning in science and the importance of assessment as a means of eliciting children's existing ideas in order to plan what to do next. She then invited her colleagues to examine the floorbook and concept maps. She challenged them to suggest suitable interventions based on the assessment evidence available. To help them understand the process of producing concept maps she asked them to draw their own using key words related to assessment that had been the theme of their term's discussions. After these had been discussed, she summarized the session and drew her colleagues' attention to the Nuffield Primary Science (1995) materials that they had in school and the link between the strategies introduced and the approach advocated within those materials.

feedback to the whole staff; introduction and prearranged contributions from other colleagues; and presentation followed by group activities and a plenary discussion. The possibilities are considerable. However, when organizing discussions it is worth bearing in mind that a group of more than seven participants is unlikely to allow for all to be actively involved. Five or six is an ideal number for a meaningful discussion. Consequently, in a large school it is better to split staff up into smaller groups and organize feedback from each group to the whole staff.

The topic or theme of the meetings might be linked to: children's learning; teaching approaches and strategies; producing or reviewing policies or schemes of work; collaborative planning; sharing practice; analysing children's work, moderation, or agreement trialing; whole school issues (assessment, special educational needs or SEN, continuity, differentiation); or auditing colleagues' subject knowledge. Alternatively subject leaders may organize the meeting as a practical workshop for colleagues, which might address: subject knowledge or skills; using commercial packages and videos; or the introduction of new resources, equipment, or materials. Visits to other schools, local education authority (LEA) centres, higher education institutions (HEIs), exhibitions, conferences, museums etc. are another good use of staff meeting time.

Task 9.1

List staff meetings in which you have played a significant role as a subject leader. For each example, identify the purpose of the meeting, the organization of the session and your role at different stages of the session. Were the purposes achieved on each occasion? How could the sessions have been improved and been more successful?

Whatever the activity, a key to its success will be thorough preparation and systematic follow-up. When planning meetings or sessions it is helpful to bear the following points (based on Waters 1996) in mind and act on them:

1. set a clear purpose for the meeting and decide how to make this explicit to participants at the outset;
2. sort out timings carefully and provide a written agenda whenever possible;
3. arrange the room in advance and choose a good place to sit so everyone can see you (with a wall rather than window behind you to help sound projection and limit distractions);
4. ensure all the necessary resources, equipment and materials are available and working in advance of the meeting;
5. consider providing refreshments and when to offer them to colleagues;
6. think about strategies that will encourage discussion and involve everyone actively (for example, get pairs or trios to discuss a key idea and share their responses);
7. plan how to introduce paperwork or documents, if appropriate (for example, give out a summary beforehand, or provide highlighter pens to encourage them to mark key sections);
8. identify others who might be involved in the session to help and provide support (for example, if a negative response from a colleague is anticipated, ask them to act as note taker);
9. be clear about what decisions the meeting needs to make and, at the end, make a summary of what has been decided, who is going to do what, by when, how, and when the issue will be revisited or reviewed;
10. decide who will produce notes or minutes of the meeting. A record, to which those present agree, is a good way of avoiding the need to rehearse discussions at a later date and provide, by including an action list, a means of checking that things get done.

An isolated meeting, or in-service session, however, is unlikely to have a significant impact on school improvement. Therefore meetings should be seen as part of an ongoing process. Consequently, making decisions about what needs doing next and who will do it is vital. A good strategy is to identify what everyone in the meeting is going to do as a consequence of the discussion, to foster the idea of school improvement being a collaborative process. For example, after the meeting in Case Study 9.1, the head teacher (who also acted as the school's assessment coordinator) agreed to compile a school portfolio of assessment evidence for pupils from R to Y6; the subject leader agreed to provide ongoing support for her colleagues as they tried out one of the strategies introduced and the other teachers agreed to try either using a floorbook or concept mapping with their classes over the next six weeks and provide an example of what they had done for the portfolio.

Working with teams of colleagues

Subject leaders may be asked, or decide, to work with smaller teams of colleagues on specific tasks. These may be year groups, departments or working parties. Task orientated teams can tackle a variety of activities, such as: developing a key stage record keeping system; organizing a whole school project, book week or environmental area; choosing a new mathematics curriculum resource. In this context, it is worth thinking about taking a more systematic approach to team work, which might involve the following stages (based on an approach advocated by the Coverdale organization; (TES 1989):

1. Allocate roles to team members – who will act as chair, scribe, time-keeper etc.?
2. Clarify the nature of the task – why does it need doing?
3. Be clear about the outcomes of the team activity – what do you want to end up with?
4. Identify criteria to evaluate the team's achievements – how will you judge whether you have been successful?
5. Collect together relevant information and ideas – what do we know/have already?
6. List specific subtasks or activities that need doing – what needs doing to achieve the goals?
7. Allocate subtasks – who is going to do what, when and how?

After this planning phase, a doing phase will probably involve individuals or subgroups going off to do their allocated tasks before the team meets again to review its successes or explore and plan ways to overcome any difficulties that have arisen.

Such an approach to group work may seem overly prescriptive, but evidence suggests that it can considerably increase the effectiveness and efficiency of teams if such an approach is adopted. Time spent in careful planning pays dividends later. It is hoped most teachers have already developed effective teamwork skills, but it may be worth reminding colleagues of the importance of active listening and responsive questioning, negotiating, clarifying, respecting others' opinions, constructive criticism etc. A good way of improving the efficiency of teams is to invite a colleague (not directly involved in the task) to observe the group processes and provide feedback at regular points, or perhaps at the end about how the team worked and the different contributions colleagues made. This can be a very revealing process.

INSET days

It is increasingly common for subject leaders to organize and deliver in-service days for their colleagues. This can be a daunting challenge, especially for those relatively new to the job, but also very satisfying. Much of what was said above about staff meetings is clearly relevant to an INSET day, but because of the time involved there is greater potential for organizing activities that can have a greater impact on colleagues. A full day on one theme or topic allows for more in-depth discussion and meaningful activities. Approaching such days in a professional and enthusiastic way will be the best way of encouraging a professional response from colleagues. INSET days provide important opportunities for regular professional development for teachers – the era of INSET days being used to clear out cupboards or to enjoy a day on 'weaving' at the end of term are past.

The key to a successful day is likely to be a variety of content and teaching strategies, providing opportunities for teachers to learn through their preferred learning style. Like children, adults have preferred learning styles. For example, according to Kolb (1976, 1984) and others (Honey and Mumford 1986), learning styles can involve activists (who prefer to learn through involvement in new experiences), reflectors (who like to stand back and ponder experiences), theorists (who prefer abstract conceptualization) and pragmatists (who like to try things out to see if they work in practice). In other words, some people prefer to learn by doing, others by reading and thinking about ideas before putting them into practice, and some through combinations of these styles. Plans should reflect these differences. Indeed, part of the preparation might include an attempt to find out more about the preferred learning styles of colleagues.

Task 9.2

Which way do you like to get the new information and ideas? Do you like to hear a lecture and have someone tell you about it? Do you like to read the new information in a book or a magazine? Do you like to see pictorial/diagrammatic sources of information? Do you like to do or to practice something to learn it? Do you like to talk with someone about a topic to understand something better? Reflect on in-service activities you have experienced recently – were there opportunities to learn in the way you preferred?

Preferred learning styles can also relate to sensory preferences. Gardner (1993) links learning styles to different intelligences, leading to the following taxonomy: good linguistic learners; good mathematical learners; good visual-spatial learners; good physical (kinaesthetic) learners; good musical (auditory) learners; good interpersonal (social) learners; and good intrapersonal (intuitive) learners. Effective learning involves learners using a range of learning styles, and so a successful in-service session should include opportunities for this and not concentrate exclusively on one style. We all know listening to someone talking at you all day is not an effective way to learn.

Thorough preparation and planning are essential for a successful INSET day and should be based on a systematic analysis of colleagues' professional needs (see Chapter 8). As we have already stressed, an INSET day run in isolation is unlikely to have a lasting impact on colleagues' practice or children's learning. Therefore, subject leaders should include in their planning how they will organize the lead-up to the day through, for example, a preparatory staff meeting, provision of background information in advance; or setting colleagues some preparatory work or activities before the day. The latter might involve colleagues in collecting examples of children's work, such as 'transactional writing', to analyse and share on the INSET day, without making too many demands of them.

Equally important is thinking, at the planning stage, of how the INSET day will be followed up. What will be the outcomes and what will colleagues be expected to do? The procedure used for staff meetings is one option, but a constructive way of concluding an INSET day is to have a few minutes when colleagues, perhaps in pairs, identify some aspect of the day that they can use to improve their practice. The subject leader can then set a date when the implementation of these action plans can be reviewed at a staff meeting (perhaps in the same pairs).This will encourage colleagues to do something as a result of the day, and encourage collaboration – an aspect of the action planning can be discussion of the support the pair can provide each other, or that they hope for from others in school. Figure 3.1 (p. 44) might be used to support this approach.

It is well worth considering the involvement of outsiders in the delivery of the day (if finances allow). This might be another, perhaps more experienced, subject leader from a local school, an LEA advisor or advisory teacher, a HEI tutor or an independent consultant. There are advantages and disadvantages to this. An advantage is the impact that an outsider can have in saying the same things the subject leader has been saying for ages. However, this is offset by the potential loss of control of the day. It is essential to negotiate the nature of the input and involvement of the external provider in detail before the event, otherwise the external provider may work to their own agenda, rather than that of the school. Using someone recommended by another school or through reputation is desirable. The benefits of a local teacher, who is also dealing with the everyday demands of the classroom can be considerable, but of course there may be supply cover costs to meet. These could be overcome by a reciprocal arrangement where subject leaders agree to offer their support to other schools at a future date.

To return to the organization of the day, plans should detail the time available for each activity or task with the subject leader seeking to keep the day on time, while retaining some flexibility for dealing with the unexpected.

A lot can be achieved in 20 minutes of small group discussion if the group is given a manageable task and keeps to it. When planning the day, the following are examples of ways in which sessions might be structured:

- full group activity or discussion – in semicircular rows for input or watching a video, in a circle for more open discussion, 'brainstorming' or review;
- small groups, pairs or trios who report back verbally, through a poster or overhead transparency;
- fish bowl – one group performs or completes a task while another group observes, and then, perhaps, swap around;
- role modelling or demonstration – for example, if exploring parental interviews, the subject leader could conduct a mock interview with a colleague in the role of a parent and the invite constructive criticism from observing colleagues;
- role play – colleagues play different roles during a discussion or activity to help them depersonalize situations and issues – has some potential difficulties attached, so needs to be used with care;
- intergroup – groups engage in competitive activities, although this may well be at odds with the values approach you are trying to encourage and therefore inappropriate;
- simultaneous activities – while one group does one thing, another group does something else and the outcomes are shared;
- options – groups or individuals choose from a range of activities or tasks;
- circus – groups move around a variety of tasks or activities;
- rainbow groups – start with each group allocated a colour and after an activity or discussion all regroup in rainbow groups to share experiences from their separate colour groups;
- change around – you change the groups for each task or activity to ensure a greater mix of ideas and avoid stagnation and/or disruptive groups forming;
- jigsaw groups – start in random groups and identify individuals with specific experience and expertise related to aspects of the task or problem under consideration. These 'experts' then form groups to work on their particular aspect before returning as pieces of the original jigsaw group to pool ideas.

Whatever structures are used, colleagues must be clear what they are expected to do, what they are expected to produce and how long they have got to do it. The subject leader's role during these activities will clearly vary according to their nature.

One of the reasons subject leaders often feel threatened by such events are the problems that can be posed by difficult individuals, in particular the member of staff who is an incessant talker and dominates small and large group discussions. The following strategies might be considered to help deal with this:

- planning the organization of tasks to minimize the opportunities for one person to do all the talking, for example get each member of the group to write down one idea and share it;

- organizing subgroups so the talker does not dominate the whole group;
- pairing the talker with another assertive member of staff or member of the senior management team;
- sitting next to the talker so that it is harder for them to catch your eye;
- asking the talker to act as scribe or chair;
- responding very positively when a less confident colleague offers a tentative idea, and inviting them to expand and lead the discussion.

The impact of INSET

Planning professional development involves an understanding of its likely impact. In Chapter 8 we introduced a model of ways in which subject leaders might provide support. Such support is intended to impact on adult learning at four levels (Joyce and Showers 1980):

- general awareness of new skills;
- organized knowledge of the concept and theory underlying the skills;
- learning of principles and skills ready for action;
- transfer and application of the new skills to the classroom and integration into the teaching repertoire.

Ideally, plans for an in-service day, its preparation and follow-up should include opportunities for learning at these levels.

Task 9.4

With reference to the discussion in Chapter 8 about supporting colleagues and the above lists, identify strategies relevant to your subject area that you could include in an in-service session to provide learning opportunities at these levels.

The work of Kinder and Harland (1991) is also helpful in informing the planning of professional development and its potential impact. Using case studies they proposed a typology of INSET outcomes (see Figure 9.1) to illustrate the impact on practice.

Their analysis indicates that first order outcomes are essential, but are not enough on their own. 'Value congruence' relates to the need for the values, underpinning the approach being advocated, to be owned by everyone involved if they are to invest in changing their practice. Consequently, in-service activities should involve making these values explicit, providing opportunities for them to be explored, and, if necessary, modified to ensure they are as congruent as possible with those of all participants.

Their second order outcomes reinforce the significance of colleagues' emotional response to the session. Feelings are important and planning an

LEVELS	OUTCOMES		
Third order	*provisionary*	*information*	*new awareness*
Second order	*motivational*	*affective*	*institutional*
First order	*value congruence*	*knowledge*	*skills*
IMPACT ON PRACTICE			

Figure 9.1 Outcomes of INSET
Source: based on Kinder and Harland 1991:161

in-service day that takes these into account will pay dividends. This might include: ensuring the activities are enjoyable; ensuring colleagues feel valued and their strengths recognized; including time for social interactions. Research by one of us into adult learning (Ritchie 1993) even indicated that the initial welcome and participants' first impressions of the setting and environment for the session can affect the impact of that session on their practice. Such factors are important.

Additionally, Kinder and Harland's typology recognizes, as we have stressed throughout this book, the importance of the institutional dimension – ensuring what is planned is set in a whole-school context and that colleagues are working together to make improvements, not in isolation. However, any typology like this is simplistic and one of the values of their case studies is that they indicate the complex interdependency of these factors. Their third order outcomes related to: giving colleagues things (ideas, advice, resources etc.); providing them with information (for example, about curriculum requirements); and raising awareness. It is relatively easy to build these into INSET plans but including the vital second and first order outcomes is much more challenging.

Evaluating INSET

Finally a systematic and valid evaluation of INSET days, and other substantive professional development opportunities for colleagues, is essential. This will have a formative purpose, helping to plan the next stage; a diagnostic purpose, helping to clarify colleagues' future learning needs; a summative purpose, helping to justify the use of resources and time involved and to identify the impact of the day on colleagues' practice. Subject leaders should identify potential audiences for the evaluation in advance of the event since this will affect the approach to be taken. It might be exclusively for the subject leader or, more likely, a report for colleagues, head teacher, governors, parents, LEA adviser, or Ofsted inspectors. Evaluation of in-service days can take a variety of forms but all are based on the following principles: colleagues should be directly involved in the process, even to the extent of planning the most appropriate way of evaluating the day; data to inform the evaluation should be collected in a variety of ways, ideally, from different sources; long term evaluation is necessary to determine changes to colleagues' practice; all the data collected should be analysed before making evaluative judgements – the temptation to make judgements based on the initial responses should be resisted.

The ongoing monitoring of the subject (see Chapter 12) provides an important source of data to inform an evaluation of the impact of INSET, but more direct and immediate approaches include:

- encouraging participants to keep a diary during the day and over the next few weeks, including significant feelings and actions;
- using fortune lines (White and Gunstone 1992) to get colleagues to plot their confidence, attitudes and feelings during the session and the follow-up period, annotating the lines with the reasons for changes – why did a colleagues' confidence suddenly go up (or down)?
- identifying a 'spotter' at the outset, to keep notes about a particular issue or factor (for example, the contribution of all colleagues in discussions, or gender issues);
- using Post-It notes as 'bricks on a wall' to allow colleagues to add their thoughts, ideas and comments throughout the day or at set points;
- inviting a governor along to monitor the day and provide you with feedback on specific issues that are identified in advance;
- keeping notes of informal discussions you have with colleagues throughout the day;
- having a follow-up staff meeting and inviting colleagues to bring evidence of changes to their practice;
- setting up a staffroom notice board for colleagues to add notes of things they have tried and the success or otherwise of them;
- inviting colleagues, at the end of the event, to discuss the sessions in pairs or small groups and give their responses to the subject leader or whole group.

We have reservations about the traditional and common approach to evaluation, which involves a brief summative questionnaire given out and filled in at the end of the day, especially if it is used in isolation. The responses might give some information about what we would call the feelgood factor, but are limited in other ways. We would also want to emphasize that the evaluation is not simply focusing on the subject leader's role as a provider, but is also encouraging everyone to reflect on their own contribution to the success, or otherwise, of the INSET. A questionnaire, if used, should include self-evaluative questions about the part an individual played – did they get actively involved in workshop activities or make contributions to group discussions?

Task 9.5

List the ways in which you have been asked to evaluate professional development activities in the past. Reflect on the strengths and weaknesses of these for you as a participant and for the provider. Can you add other strategies to the list above?

Making presentations to others

Subject leaders are increasingly being expected to make formal presentations to groups other than their colleagues in school. These might be to governors or parents, or to groups of teachers from other schools, perhaps at a meeting of the local cluster group. Although teachers are effectively giving presentations to groups of pupils every day, the challenge of talking to a large group of adults is far more daunting. Therefore, before we leave the theme of working with groups, we offer some advice on planning and delivering formal talks or presentations to groups. This will apply equally to those made to colleagues (at staff meetings or during INSET days) or external groups. Based on our experience, we would suggest the following (although we have not always practised what we preach):

- plan the talk thoroughly in advance. Produce a concept map or brainstorm of the points to be covered, select the key ideas (not too many) and supporting statements, organize these into a logical structure. Take account of what the group already knows;
- use ideas written on cards as aide-mémoire; it is very hard to use a script or to memorize a talk and it can end up sounding boring and uninspiring;
- practise the talk with a friend to check timing and structure;
- prepare the venue in advance, considering warmth, light, position of seating and point of delivery. Standing behind a desk (or even a lectern) can give a sense of security, but conveys a more formal sense to the audience;
- talk to a colleague while the group assembles or, if it helps, welcome individuals as they arrive. Avoid looking nervous or disorganized and having to do things at the last moment;
- take time before beginning. Wait until the audience is settled and quiet, take up a position so that eye contact can be maintained without obscuring the overhead projector (OHP) or other visual aids, if used. Try to look and sound relaxed;
- outline the structure and content of the talk in the introduction, and summarize the key points at the end;
- produce high quality audiovisual aids such as overhead transparencies. It shows the input has been taken seriously and aids communication. However, avoid reading out long lists and quotations from an overhead transparency that the audience can read. Talk around the points on the

transparency or why the quotation is significant. A video clip can be a good way of adding interest to a talk;
- be enthusiastic and support ideas with good, but brief, examples from personal or colleagues' practice.
- don't give out handouts during the talk unless it essential that they are read at that time. Most people do not find it easy to read and listen and distributing papers can be very disruptive. However, a sheet of key points given out before starting, with space for participants to add their own notes can be valuable. Include information about where they can find out more about the ideas if they wish, for example books in the staff library;
- avoid being a roving talker. It is easier to concentrate on a speaker who stands still and does not fidget;
- speak conversationally, but project the voice so it can be heard by everyone (check, if necessary). Some speakers focus on a friend in the audience, or a 'nodder', and talk to them as an individual. Avoid jokes (unless you are good at telling them) and patronizing remarks or anything that might be misconstrued by individuals. Constantly monitor the audience for signs of incomprehension and respond if any are noted;
- try and build interactive elements into the structure, for example, asking the audience for examples or perhaps a five-minute break in the input in which pairs discuss a question and contribute their thoughts;
- avoid jargon or too many acronyms, especially when talking to parents, governors or other non-teacher groups;
- bring the talk to a conclusion without rushing the last few points and make sure to keep to time (especially at the end of the day or at an evening meeting);
- invite questions but anticipate beforehand what they might be, or ask a friendly colleague to suggest some that might arise;
- accept that each individual will take away a unique interpretation or understanding of what is said and that none of them will have an identical understanding to the speaker – however good the presentation was!

For subject leaders really looking to impress the audience, and willing to take a risk with technology, presentation software like Powerpoint (from Microsoft) can add a new dimension to talks. However, at the end of the day, whatever strategies or technologies are used, it will be personal enthusiasm and attitude that will probably have the biggest impact on the audience.

Summary

Subject leadership involves a range of social skills. This chapter has focused on subject leaders as they work in social contexts with their colleagues and others. We have examined the part subject leaders can play in planning, implementing and evaluating learning opportunities for their colleagues during staff meetings, afterschool workshops and in-service days. In all cases, the particular event or session has been seen as a part of a bigger whole. School improvement can be conceptualized through the metaphor of the school staff going on a journey. Such events as we have explored in this chapter are small parts of the journey and only significant when seen as staging posts on the way to greater goals. In Chapter 8, parallels were drawn between pupils' learning and adult learning. Those parallels are also evident in the content of this chapter. Classroom learning occurs in a social context and individuals' learning is affected by their interactions with peers and their teacher. When working with groups of colleagues, their learning (or professional development) is similarly affected by peers and the provider (in this case the subject leader). Learning for children and adults is a complex process, involving emotional as well as cognitive dimensions. This theme has also featured in our discussion – colleagues must be motivated, and want to learn; they have to make an emotional commitment to their professional development. Subject leaders need to recognize this and provide support for colleagues in such a way that, we hope, they may even enjoy the experience of learning as they improve their practice.

Part IV

RESOURCES

10

MANAGING RESOURCES

Introduction

Resources – time, money, people, space, materials and equipment – are limited in every school but, depending on the overall situation, the actual level of resourcing for subjects varies considerably both within and between schools. Given this, one of the tasks for subject leaders is to secure an appropriate level of resources and to find ways in which the best use can be made of whatever resources are available. Although the days when the main task of the subject leader was to keep the stock cupboard tidy are gone, the organization and management of resources remains a vital part of a subject leader's job. It is an area in which a new subject leader can make an impact quite quickly without too much conflict. Helping colleagues to find appropriate materials provides practical support, which is very much appreciated and can be done quite quickly, whereas many of the issues we discuss elsewhere in the book take more time and have greater potential for conflict. The management of resources, as with everything else, requires careful planning, implementation, monitoring and evaluation to ensure that they are being used effectively and the school is getting value for money. In this chapter we look at issues related to money, people, space, materials and equipment, while Chapter 11 considers the challenge of managing time effectively.

Money

Since the 1990s subject leaders have become more aware of and more involved in handling budgets. Many, for the first time, are responsible for an allocation of money that they are to use to cover the cost of running their subject each year. This may be as little as £50 or over £1000. The exact figure will depend on the school priorities, the overall budget, the subject area and, in many ways unfortunately, on the historical pattern of allocations – 'English always gets £x, so it should have it this year'. Although subject leaders may not make the final decisions in setting the school budget they do have a role to play in ensuring that each subject area gets a fair share of the available resources needed to provide an appropriate curriculum for the children.

It is beyond the scope of this book to go into financial planning and management in detail (see e.g. Knight 1993). If they are to get the best out of whatever money there is available, however, subject leaders need to be clear about the mechanisms by which funding can be obtained, to be able to prepare a budget and account for the money that has been spent. The ways in which schools allocate money for different subjects varies considerably but increasingly funds for supporting the curriculum are being made available following discussions with subject leaders and in line with the priorities of the school development plan. Ideally the procedure for this allocation is set out in advance and subject leaders should work to meet its requirements. Most important will be the negotiations with the head teacher in order to establish priorities, especially when new initiatives and additional demands, such as individual education plans (IEPs) for children with learning difficulties, are involved. Preliminary discussions are important so that new ideas can be anticipated as part of the overall budget. Inevitably more money for one subject means less for something else and the head teacher needs to be prepared for this. Negotiations with the head teacher are particularly important if he or she retains total control of the budget.

In addition to money that is made available through the school's annual budget, there are additional sources of funding which are becoming more readily available. We have examples of subject leaders and their schools obtaining money from their parent–teacher associations, sponsorship from local businesses (see Chapter 7), TTA research grants (e.g. TTA 1998c), subject association initiatives (e.g. the pupil–researcher initiative in science; see Harrison and Mannion 1998), links with the local Training and Enterprise Councils (TECs) and through various European funded projects (e.g. Socrates and Comenius programmes, which encourage co-operation between European institutions; the Comenius programme for the promotion of cooperation in education at all levels is a section of the overall Socrates programme). Obviously there are conditions to be met and there is competition for the money that is available, but a carefully thought-out application can often provide the necessary funding to help do something that would not have been possible otherwise.

Key to successful financial management is a well planned and presented budget that sets out what is required and potential sources of money. This in turn is based on a clear understanding of priorities. In drawing up such a budget, allowance has to be made for the *maintenance* and *development* of the subject. The former will include necessary materials and equipment that are usually classed as consumables (e.g. paper, paints, batteries etc.) that will be used within the year and capital (e.g. a new set of books or scheme, set of artefacts etc.) that would be expected to last a number of years. The development of the subject requires the injection of new resources in some form and perhaps some guarantee of funding beyond a single year. This may involve the purchase of some new equipment for the first time, staff development or supply cover to release the subject leader to work with colleagues. Thus it is necessary to think ahead and negotiate the necessary guarantees for funding beyond the current year.

One of the difficulties for subject leaders in drawing up a budget is that the total investment is not always clear and does not necessarily come out of 'their money'. Thus it is essential to know what the budget is to cover. For example a few subject leaders are given a total budget that must pay for everything from the drawing pins to the supply cover used in their subject. More commonly, and more appropriately, subject leaders are allocated funding to cover the consumables and agreed capital items but supply cover and staff development are dealt with separately. Nevertheless it is important that subject leaders make sure that the funding they need is available when required.

Having got the money it is essential to spend it wisely and to monitor it. Although much of the administrative work might be done by the secretary, subject leaders are responsible for the money they have been allocated. Thus they need to keep up to date with the accounts, progress of orders and so on to ensure that the money is used to best effect. This may include: taking advantage of, but not infringing, LEA purchasing agreements; negotiating discounts with suppliers; following up on delivery dates; and making sure that invoices are received and paid. If an order is not going to be met then it could be cancelled and the money used for something else. Finally subject leaders need to check that accounts are correct and may, from time to time, audit the usage of materials and evaluate the usefulness of purchases and services received.

People

Although subject leaders rarely have line management responsibilities, they do need to consider how best to use the expertise of colleagues and others. Essentially how subject leaders enlist the support of others in order to get things done is an extension to the development of the professional relationships we have discussed in Chapters 3 and 7. The success of such ventures will depend on how well subject leaders can negotiate with and motivate others to get involved. Auditing the range of knowledge and skills others have to offer might be a first step but it is then necessary to find ways of making use of the help available. An open request for people to do something can be unproductive, but an approach to help with a specific well thought out idea is often more successful. For example a colleague, who belongs to a conservation group and could be the best person to lead discussions to prepare an environmental topic, might respond to a direct request but might not volunteer. Beyond the direct use of expertise subject leaders can make a significant contribution to the development of their subject (and the school) by finding imaginative ways of increasing 'people time'. We have referred, elsewhere in this book, to ways in which support might come from colleagues, classroom assistants, students, parents, grandparents, HEIs, secondary schools, artists and actors in residence, community engineers, link scientists etc.

Simply putting additional bodies into a classroom does not automatically increase the effectiveness of the teaching and learning going on there. Therefore it is essential that everyone knows what they are trying to achieve and what they are supposed to be doing. We have discussed elsewhere ways of supporting colleagues but, despite the immense difficulties, efforts should be made to ensure that all helpers involved with children's learning receive some support and training. For most helpers it is the class teacher who will talk to them on a day to day basis but the subject leader should know what the helper is doing and ensure that the class teacher provides the necessary information. Ideally some kind of agreed guidance should be available, applying to all aspects of the curriculum, to which particular subject advice can be added to cover issues such as safety.

Materials

For many subject leaders this is the aspect of their job with which they are most familiar and with which they are most closely involved on a day to day basis. It almost goes without saying that effective teaching and learning requires appropriate resources to be available. Therefore subject leaders need to be fully aware of what is needed (both those things that are essential as well as those that might be desirable), what is available in school and what is still required. This requires them to be up to date with what materials and equipment are available, costs, and suppliers. Much of this information can be obtained from catalogues, attendance at conferences and exhibitions and from advice given by advisers and subject associations. Management of resources, however, requires a more systematic approach than has often been adopted in the past.

If it does not already exist, a list of the books, materials and equipment in the school related to the subject should be drawn up following an audit involving all members of staff. This should be compared against a list of the things that are needed to ensure the requirements of the National Curriculum can be met. A wish list can then be produced, indicating the things that are still needed as essential, desirable and as luxuries. This will allow subject leaders to plan for the acquisition of resources over a number of years. Such a major process does not need to be carried out every year but a system is needed to identify what is to be replaced and for suggestions as to what might be used to supplement the existing resources. A resources log readily available in the staffroom would meet this requirement. Subject leaders should work towards having a running list of resources to be acquired, thus helping them to take advantage of any opportunity for getting additional items.

Having identified what is wanted is only the first step. The next is to examine the range of products that are on offer. For some things it may be simply a matter of finding the cheapest supplier; for others it is essential to spend time evaluating the materials carefully. Investment in a major piece of equipment or a new published scheme is a significant undertaking that will influence what happens in the classroom for a number of years. Ideally other colleagues should be consulted before the decision to purchase is made. Although it involves some work, it can be very beneficial to organize an exhibition of books and equipment, perhaps in collaboration with other schools or the LEA, in order to provide an opportunity to inspect the different products. Increasingly electronic forms of information and sources of resource materials need to be addressed by all subject leaders. The advent of initiatives such as the National Grid for Learning (NGfL) and educational websites adds a whole new area of resources to be explored.

There is no profit in spending time identifying resources and carefully selecting them if they are not used. Thus thought must be given to the storage, accessibility and availability of the resources in school. Exactly how this will be achieved most effectively will depend on the particular school, its size, layout of buildings and storage space available as well as the overall approach to teaching and learning. Thus, as with many other areas of responsibility, subject leaders will need to work within the practices adopted by the school as a whole. Subject leaders need to get agreement as to which materials will be kept in individual classrooms and which will be kept as part of a central store. In some subject areas, the most effective approach is to make up 'topic boxes' which can be taken to wherever they are needed. It is important to ensure that everything is clearly labelled and that it is replaced after use. Although it takes time to set up a new system, there are usually benefits in terms of more efficient use of time once it is put into operation. Whatever system is used, the underlying criteria should be to ensure the most efficient use of the resources that are available.

One of the reasons why resources are not used is that some colleagues do not know how to use them to best effect. Therefore it is not enough to tell everyone that the materials have been bought; it is necessary to provide some instruction and opportunities to try them out. This is particularly true for information and communications equipment and software. Large sums of money have been and will be invested in providing such resources to meet demands for such skills. This is not simply a job for the ICT subject leader. It is part of the responsibility of all subject leaders to ensure that effective use is made of ICT in all subject areas. Case Study 10.1 illustrates many of the issues involved in the management of resources. Although in a relatively favourable position, Steve had some difficult decisions to make concerning strategies that would help get maximum benefit out of the large investment that was to be made in the equipment.

Case Study 10.1 Resources

Steve works in an inner city school and has been teaching for eight years. He is subject leader for geography and information and communications technology (ICT). As part of the school development plan he has been asked to update the ICT facilities and a budget has been allocated. This he sees as a priority because it is such a big job and therefore for much of the year he is only keeping geography ticking over.

Steve knew that there were some computers in the school but wasn't sure exactly how many were used nor what software was considered helpful. He therefore undertook an audit of all hardware and software in the school, finding a BBC computer that everyone had forgotten about. By means of a checklist that he designed, Steve asked everyone to indicate what use they made of the computers, which software they used and found helpful, what other ICT equipment they used and what experience they had of computers, video cameras etc. outside school. He felt this would help him try to prioritize what to buy and to what extent it would be used. It also indicated which of his colleagues he might be able to call on for support and who he would need to work with in order to get them using the equipment.

From this information Steve felt that it was realistic to aim to get at least one computer into every classroom within the year and if money was available, he could increase the number the following year. The overriding priority he set was that he would like everyone to be using the computer for something on a regular basis – it was the only way they could meet what was set out in the policy and scheme of work. Therefore he felt that an important factor in the decision as to what machines and software to buy was whether or not colleagues felt comfortable with them. He prepared a plan, which he discussed with the head who was happy with it, but Steve could not use the supplier he wanted because of LEA purchasing agreements. He circulated the plan for discussion at the next staff meeting, where it was agreed.

Steve then spent some time talking to individual members of staff to agree which machines and software they would have to begin with and enlisted the support of those colleagues with some experience of computers to pair up with those that hadn't. This arrangement did not work as well as he hoped but in some cases it was very successful. As the new machines arrived Steve arranged workshops to help colleagues get used to the equipment before transferring them into the classrooms. Steve is in the middle of the implementation of his plan, which is generally going well but he feels that he had misjudged the time it would take.

Making the most of the classroom

'Weren't those displays wonderful?' is a comment often heard in relation to a good teacher. Although it does not follow that impressive displays make a good teacher, it is generally true that good teachers in primary schools tend to make effective use of displays. This is not surprising because they recognize the importance of creating a classroom that is not only pleasing to look at but also provides stimulation and reinforcement of the teaching and learning that goes on there. Clearly every teacher has a responsibility to maintain a lively classroom that provides stimulation and encourages children to learn. It is important that there is variety within the school, thus providing children with a range of experiences.

Given that every teacher is not an expert in every subject – hence the need for subject leaders – support and advice is often welcome on ways to improve the classroom, organize lessons and on new environments that can be exploited to engage children's thinking and help them develop their understanding and skills. Thus subject leaders can usefully look at their colleagues' classrooms from the point of view of their subjects to consider the opportunities and constraints they offer. For example, is the arrangement of the furniture conducive to carrying out practical science activities or does it allow children easy access to the sink for cleaning art equipment? A fresh eye can often make useful suggestions. Subject leaders might also help in the setting up of subject-focused displays, possibly involving an interactive exploration table that invites children to do something or think about what they see. The book corner could be stocked temporarily with a selection of materials on a particular topic (these can often be obtained from the library service).

Classrooms should be aesthetically pleasing, stimulate children and display their work to a high standard. However, it has to be remembered that it 'belongs' to the class teacher and their class. Therefore subject leaders cannot dictate what takes place but should set an example through the way in which they use their classrooms, and other areas of the school, to enhance the teaching and learning in their subjects.

Task 10.1

Walk round your school and identify good examples of how your subject has been enhanced by your colleagues through displays of different kinds. In what ways do you think you could improve the situation?

School grounds and other places of interest

There is great potential to use school grounds as a means of enhancing children's learning experiences which could be exploited by subject leaders. Many schools have set up 'outside classrooms' as a whole school project providing children with opportunities to involve themselves in activities such as the observation of living things (as a stimulus for science, art, English), mathematics trails, games, quiet areas for reading and gardening. Although it is not possible for every school to have designated areas for work outside, there are opportunities that can be exploited in most subjects and that are probably best developed through collaboration between all the subject leaders.

Beyond the school gates there are almost limitless opportunities for extending children's experiences and opportunities for learning. The list of places to visit is endless (e.g. museums, zoos, farms, heritage centres, airports, fire stations etc.). However they need to be carefully planned and organized. The purpose of such visits should be clear to everyone and it is for the relevant subject leader to provide advice on the activities that might be appropriate and, where relevant, alternative venues for such work. The subject leader's advice might also extend to the type of work the children could do as preparation and follow-up to the visit.

Summary

The management of resources is one of the key areas of responsibility for subject leaders, requiring them to 'identify appropriate resources for the subject and ensure that they are used efficiently, effectively and safely' (TTA 1998a). In this chapter we have examined the way in which this might be done in relation to people, money, materials and space and have emphasized the importance of:

- identifying the resources needed (essential, desirable and luxuries);
- evaluating the potential of materials to meet the needs (schemes, equipment etc.);
- alternative sources of materials etc.;
- storage, distribution, allocation of resources;
- maintenance and replacement of resources, especially ICT etc.;
- currency of resources and their replacement; and
- production of resources.

11

MANAGING TIME

Introduction

Everyone is under pressure to get things done but there are never enough hours in the day and it is too easy to use time as an excuse. The reality is that there is only a certain amount of time available to meet the conflicting demands on that time. This gives rise to tension, stress, and, ultimately if nothing is done to ease the situation, breakdown of the individual and/or the organization. The position of subject leaders in primary schools is one that probably has more than its fair share of tension and conflicting interests, in particular that between being an effective subject leader and a good class teacher. Thus we need to be clear what the demands are, find ways of reducing the conflicts, and develop strategies for using the time available more effectively.

The need for time – clarifying the issue

Time, or rather lack of it, is probably the one thing that has been referred to by subject leaders in every conversation we have had with them about their jobs. It is seen by some as the sole reason preventing them from making progress in developing their subject area; as one subject leader said, 'There are no other major difficulties in [subject leaders] carrying out their responsibilities'. While comments of this nature are commonplace, they are not very helpful in trying to identify the cause of the time difficulty. We fully acknowledge that the time constraints are real and severely inhibiting for some subject leaders all of the time and for all subject leaders some of the time. It is essential, however, to take a little time to try and clarify what is behind the concerns about lack of time. This can be considered in two ways.

First, we can explore how subject leaders are using their time and the problems facing them. In Chapter 1 (Table 1.3) we indicated the time spent by some subject leaders on different categories of task in a week. Subsequent discussions with the subject leaders indicated that, despite the substantial time spent on subject leader tasks over and above their work as a class teacher:

- it is not possible to carry out every aspect of the job and some tasks inevitably are left undone;
- too much of the time for talking to colleagues ends up being a snatched two or three minute conversation in the corridor or on playground duty and only rarely a sustained discussion;
- increasingly subject leaders have curriculum management time but little of it, if any, is during the school day to work alongside colleagues;
- much of the work has to be done at home in the evening, if tasks are to be completed;
- time to carry out tasks is not guaranteed so it is difficult to plan ahead;
- there is a constant conflict of responsibilities particularly with the demands of being a class teacher and meeting requests from children.

Thus it would seem that not only is there a need for more time overall but there is also a need for blocks of time of appropriate length and frequency which are, as far as possible, guaranteed and free from other distractions.

Second, we can try to set out what subject leaders need time for. Demands on the time of most, if not all, subject leaders will originate from five main sources:

- their responsibilities as subject leader;
- their responsibilities as class teachers;
- any additional responsibilities in school, for example, deputy head teacher, governor, subject leader for other curriculum areas and mentor for newly qualified teachers (NQTs)
- their own personal development; and
- their own personal life.

In addition to the tensions that exist between each of these areas there are competing demands within each of them. Thus in global terms subject leaders need time for all of these things and it is this requirement that sets the context for any consideration of ways in which time can be used more effectively. Within these broad parameters we can identify more specific demands on time as set out in Table 11.1.

The lists included in the table are by no means exhaustive. They serve only to illustrate the complex nature of what is involved trying to manage time more effectively. The important thing is to take some time, on a regular basis, to look at the overall picture and identify what the demands are, where those demands are coming from and what factors prevent the best use of the time that is available.

Table 11.1 Demands on subject leaders' time

Responsibilities as subject leader include:
- consultations with head teacher;
- retaining the vision and overview through thinking and planning time;
- developing and preparing documentation (policies and schemes of work etc.);
- meetings;
- supporting colleagues both formally and informally outside the classroom;
- working alongside colleagues in the classroom;
- observing teaching and learning in other parts of the school;
- checking and organizing resources;
- administrative tasks such as ordering materials;
- outside visits.

Responsibilities as class teacher include:
- planning and preparing lessons;
- organizing the classroom;
- marking work;
- completing children's reports;
- responding to children's needs.

Additional responsibilities might include:
- subject leader tasks for another area of the curriculum;
- oversight of the curriculum as deputy head teacher;
- governors meetings and subcommittee work;
- counselling newly qualified teachers and students;
- organizing the school play.

Own personal and professional development might include:
- attendance on courses;
- own research writing;
- membership of subject organization/associations;
- contacts with other subject leaders, including cluster group meetings;
- discussions with LEA advisers and inspectors.

Personal life might include:
- family commitments;
- holidays;
- property maintenance;
- own interests/sport.

Task 11.1

Using the categories in Table 11.1 as a starting point draw up your own version of the table to set out the demands that you have on your time currently. Add a third column to your table and against each demand indicate whether you feel you are meeting the demand: very well, satisfactorily, not very well or not at all. For those you feel you are not meeting very well or not at all consider why you feel this is so and what you might do about it.

Meeting the challenge

It is relatively easy to recognize that 'time' is a problem but it is more difficult to accept that first, in reality there are far more demands than there is time available; second, even if everything could be done, it cannot be done perfectly and can only be done as well as the circumstances at the time allow; third, that there are no magic formulas to managing time, no one does it perfectly, but the necessary skills can be developed in order to do so more effectively; and fourth, a lack of time is not necessarily the reason for not doing something, it could just be an excuse for not having thought through the tasks and issues clearly in the first place. The solution to the problem of 'time' is not simply having more of it, rather it is about using what time is available more efficiently and effectively. It is always much better to be able to demonstrate that the time available is being used well and then being able to show what any additional time would be used for than simply to say 'I need more time'.

Setting priorities

Whether the attempts to make better use of time are at the school or the personal level, one of the key steps is the need to set the priorities and plan activities to meet them. In the same way that we discussed planning as taking place at different levels (see Chapter 4) there are different categories of priority that need to be reconciled. In particular subject leaders will need to balance personal, professional and organizational priorities and, within each of these areas, consider what are the long, medium and short term requirements. Many of the overall priorities will be established as part of the planning processes we referred to in Chapter 4, but these need to be implemented. The key distinctions subject leaders need to establish are, first, between those things that are urgent and those that are important and, second, between those things that they can or should do and those that can or should be done by someone else.

One simple approach to setting priorities is to combine the use of a simple timeline or critical path diagram with a coding system to indicate the level of importance attached to a task. The timeline or critical pathway sets out when particular jobs need to be completed and establishes intermediate and final deadlines. This process is particularly helpful in identifying which tasks depend on the completion of others. Once the timescale for the tasks is established, each task can be then assigned to a level of importance as follows:

1 these activities are essential and must be completed and/or progressed if targets are to be met and timing is of the essence;
2 these tasks need to be completed as part of the targets but the timing is less critical, that is, no one is depending on its completion in the short term;
3 these are interesting activities but not essential to completing the job or meeting targets and so can be left or fitted in if time is available when 1 and 2 activities have been completed;

4 these are lowest priority or irrelevant to the job and so should be passed on to someone else or dumped.

Taking the process of setting priorities seriously, within the overall agreed targets for the school and the subject, should help in addressing perhaps the major difficulty faced by subject leaders. This was summed up by one subject leader who wrote,

> Deciding which is my priority – teaching my class or carrying out duties of science [subject leader]. This is of course linked to the factor of time. I believe my prime concern *must* be the general teaching of my class – but this does lead to a conflict as I must also be an effective [subject leader]. This, I find, leads to stress if one is at all conscientious. The only solution is more time but this can only be given at the expense of time with my class. This is detrimental to the well-being and progress of the class, especially if they are very young. I find I don't know the answer to this.
> (Bell 1990: 216)

Unfortunately there is no easy answer to this conflict nor to the tensions felt by subject leaders who are responsible for more than one area of the curriculum. What is important, however, is the need to step back and try to look at the whole picture when setting priorities. As a class teacher it is the children in the class who have highest priority but as a subject leader it is all of the children in the school who should benefit. Both are very important and therefore it is necessary to agree the balance between the two with the head teacher. Similarly the choice of which area of the curriculum to focus on needs to be agreed and the decision accepted as a given unless there is a change in circumstances.

Time as a whole school issue

We cannot emphasize too strongly that improvements in the use of time cannot be brought about by an individual in isolation. Individuals can make a difference to the way in which they use their time but this can only happen in the context of the school as an organization and the outside pressures on them. As one subject leader said, 'I can manage my time, it's everyone else that gets in the way!' (Bell 1990: 216). Every school needs to step back and try to address the 'problem' of time as an organization in order to establish clear parameters within which everyone can work. Advice sent to headteachers by the DfEE (1998d) provides guidelines that aim to help schools cut down on the red tape and contribute to more effective use of time.

'The process [of school development planning] was said to provide a structure and coherence to planning which was logical and "common sense" and which led to a more efficient use of time'(MacGilchrist *et al.* 1995:78). School development plans, although very helpful, will not automatically solve the problems of time. They can be overambitious, setting unrealistic targets and timescales that only add to the pressures, further compounding the problem.

Case Study 11.1 Using time effectively

After a year in post as head teacher of a relatively new two form entry primary school, Wendy felt that her staff were under a lot of pressure. She called a staff meeting to outline her concerns and everyone agreed that the big problem was 'time'. They decided to do something about it as a staff. Everyone made suggestions of how they could save time but they did not feel they were making progress. Over a period of weeks Wendy spoke informally to everyone and a further meeting was held at which Wendy, in order to ease some of the pressures, proposed some simple ground rules that should be adhered to as far as possible. These were based on:

- respect and trust of colleagues' use of time so, for example meetings should start and end on time and if, for example, a subject leader said they were spending the lunch-hour putting together some equipment boxes then other colleagues should not, unless it is really urgent, interrupt;
- improving lines of communications and giving more thought to the most appropriate method of communication to be used;
- the use of agreed systems for different processes such as recording and reporting children's work as well as the booking of the hall or television.

Overall they were attempting to build a culture in which the quality of collaboration was improved by everyone working towards the same end in ways which were compatible and not constantly pulling in different directions. Although it is early days, the adoption of the 'ground rules' seem to have eased the pressures somewhat and most of the staff feel less time is wasted.

On the other hand, well thought-out school development plans to which everyone has been party will set out realistic aims, targets, priorities and timescales for what the school hopes to achieve within a given period of time. It is possible therefore to agree allocations of time for all the processes needed to support the developments, including time for planning, staff development and non-contact time for subject leaders to support colleagues. Thus the school development plan can provide the framework in which, as subject leaders and class teachers, everyone can make their own contribution, set out their own targets, priorities, timescales and deadlines.

In addition to the contribution a good school development plan can make, a review of other aspects of the school as an organization and community can also provide benefits. Case Study 11.1 illustrates how teachers in one school felt that time could be used more efficiently and effectively if everyone worked towards recognizing that there is a complex variety of demands on each individual's time.

One specific problem that needs to be addressed as a whole school issue is that of non-contact curriculum management time for subject leaders. It is recognized that in order to carry out their job effectively, subject leaders need non-contact time (e.g. Ofsted 1994, 1995b, 1996a). Unfortunately it is not easily arranged in many schools because of staffing levels and other difficulties. Despite this, many schools do manage to make time available through a variety of devices, such as use of a 'floating teacher' when finances allow, doubling up of classes, assembly time, and heads or deputies with non-teaching time covering for classes. Key to the success of such arrangements is that there is a clear agreed purpose, planned in advance and carefully monitored. An increase in non-contact time is not the complete solution, however, because other colleagues are unlikely to be available for consultation or collaboration at the same time (Webb and Vulliamy 1996).

Personal management of time

It is very easy to look busy and yet achieve very little in relation to the targets that have been set. If, despite having carried out the overall planning and set some priorities, some attention is not given to the use of time on a day to day basis then a great deal of effort and time will have been wasted. Thus, having identified what should be done and mapped out the priorities overall, the plans must be put into practice on a day to day basis in order to ensure that the agreed targets are met.

Exactly how this is achieved will depend on each individual and their preferred style of working. The important thing is that some time should be taken to plan and organize workloads. Failure to stand back and look at the wider picture will result in permanently playing 'catch-up'. Modification of work patterns can help to avoid 'catch-up', to cut out time wasting, to ensure the important things get done on time, to manage the flow of work and to remain free from stress. Useful strategies include:

- a diary or organizer that is considered to be an action planner and not simply something for recording appointments. Time is allocated for the various tasks and noted in the diary to ensure that there is space to do all the jobs that need to be done. This requires setting start and finish times with realistic estimations of the time required to complete the task to an acceptable level for the purpose in hand. This does not mean that everything will be done perfectly but things will get done. It is also important to build in and retain an element of 'me-time' for reflection.
- a routine of reviewing the tasks for each day. This requires listing the tasks, allocating priorities, times and the order of implementation. Uncompleted tasks should be carried over to the following day and reviewed alongside the new tasks that come along. Obviously some degree of flexibility needs to be allowed but it is important to try to keep to the schedule set out.

- projects, how ever small, need to be planned out and a critical path determined so that everyone who is involved knows the timescale and sequence of the necessary activities and where their own contribution fits in. On completion of the plan the action points need to be built into the school and individuals' diaries so the time is allocated for their completion.

The temptation to stop planning the use of time as the pressure of work increases must be resisted because it is precisely at these times that a few minutes spent planning can save significant amounts of time later and, more importantly, help to keep things in perspective.

Children's time

Although in this chapter we have concentrated on the way in which subject leaders and their colleagues might work to make better use of their time, it is important to remember that time is a resource that is available for children's learning. It is therefore an integral part of subject leaders' jobs to help manage the time available for children to engage with their subjects. As we indicated in Chapter 5 one of the elements in a scheme of work should be an indication of the amount of time that each unit of work should take. This is not to say that this is the total amount of time that will be spent on the subject area. In some schools the total will be higher because elements of the subject are covered in other areas of the curriculum while in a few schools it is likely that the time allocated in the scheme of work is not used. Thus each school should keep under review the amount of curriculum time that is available and the proportions that are used for the different subject areas. Subject leaders should contribute to this exercise and need to examine the outcomes carefully in order to evaluate whether or not the time available for their curriculum areas is appropriate.

Managing such an exercise can be difficult and a potential source of conflict, especially if individual subject leaders become possessive and see it as a competition to get as much time as possible for 'their' subjects. A time audit of the kind we have in mind would set out to:

- make a realistic assessment of the total amount of time available for each of the full range of activities that take place in the school each week throughout the year, including assemblies, collective worship, end of key stage tests, breaks and lunchtimes, concerts, extracurricular activities;
- identify the total amount of time spent on covering the curriculum as a whole and for each element of it;
- examine for each curriculum area, including ICT, the way in which the time for it is distributed, for example is it all accounted for in time dedicated to the subject or is it split across several topics of work?
- consider, within each curriculum area, the amount of time that is devoted to each part of the programme of study, for example within English how much time is taken up with reading and writing as opposed to speaking

and listening or within science how much time is used for living things as opposed to materials?
- take the opportunity to identify where cross-curricular matters such as spiritual and moral values, heath education, citizenship, industrial and economic awareness, equal opportunities and multicultural education are dealt with.

An audit such as this is a major undertaking but necessary from time to time. It allows schools to address the question 'How can we fit everything in?' with some confidence. It has to be remembered that there are various requirements as to the amount of time that must be devoted to particular aspects of the curriculum and other activities, such as the literacy and numeracy hours, homework, core subjects and foundation subjects. These all have to be taken into consideration as does the need to resist narrowing the curriculum and 'teaching to the test'.

Analysis of the information and the evaluation of the existing practice will need to be taken at a whole school level but as part of the process each subject leader should examine the evidence relating to their area of responsibility and ask the following questions:

- Is the overall time allocated appropriate to the demands of the subject as part of a wider curriculum?
- Is the distribution of the time suitable to allow for the necessary balance of material, progression and revisiting of the concepts and the development of the necessary skills?
- Is the coverage of the programmes of study balanced and links made with other relevant areas of the curriculum?
- Overall is the time allocation and distribution able to provide the necessary quality of learning experiences for the children in this area of the curriculum?
- Is the time that is available being used most effectively by everyone teaching the subject?

Answers to these questions will help to provide indications for subject leaders as to the types of action they need to take to improve the overall quality of teaching and learning and to ensure that the time children spend at school is well spent and not wasted.

Summary

The effective and efficient use of time, which we have addressed in this chapter, is one of the biggest challenges facing subject leaders but there are no easy solutions. By asking the following questions and acting on their own responses subject leaders should be able to make better use of the time they have available.

1. What am I trying to achieve in terms of the whole school, my responsibilities as subject leader and in the other aspects of my life? Only by having a clear view of the purpose of their job and setting realistic targets can subject leaders start to be effective.
2. What do I spend my time doing and what do I need time for? Unless subject leaders are clear about how they use their time and what still needs to be done they cannot really start to set priorities.
3. What are my priorities and what do I need to do to meet these? Subject leaders cannot do everything and therefore must know what has to be done and when in order to achieve their targets.
4. What are the things that stop me carrying out the tasks identified as priorities? Sometimes circumstances are outside the control of subject leaders and events interfere with their plans, but they can reduce the impact of the things they do have control over.
5. What strategies can I implement in order to use my time more effectively and efficiently? Having identified what can be done subject leaders must do it and work in a disciplined fashion to follow the principles they have established for making better use of their time.

Part V

CONTRIBUTING TO SCHOOL IMPROVEMENT

12

MONITORING AND EVALUATION

Introduction

The final section of this book addresses the contribution that subject leaders should make to processes of school improvement. This chapter returns to the theme of monitoring, introduced in Chapter 3 with an emphasis on auditing a situation at a particular point in time. The present discussion will focus on monitoring as an ongoing process in which subject leaders should be constantly engaged to enable them to evaluate the success of what is happening in their subjects in order to make plans about how to improve the current situation. Any improvements, of course, should be aimed at improving the quality of pupils' learning and achievements. Monitoring in most primary school contexts will inevitably be a responsibility that subject leaders share with the head teacher, deputy head teacher, and, to some extent, with governors. The head teacher will have the authority, and possibly opportunities, for monitoring that are unlikely to be available to subject leaders.

Monitoring learning

The success of a school, and of a subject leader, will be dependent on the achievements of pupils in the subject. Consequently, subject leaders need to monitor the learning that goes on to provide evidence that allows them, and others, to judge the degree of this success. By doing this, subject leaders will also be able to make planning decisions that are informed by evidence rather than impression. What children have learnt is different from what they have experienced. This needs to be recognized when planning the sort of monitoring that is appropriate. Later, we will consider the monitoring of teachers' plans and class records – these will give some indication of the content covered and the experiences that the children may have been offered. It will not provide evidence of what they have learnt, nor how. Insights into pupils' achievements require more direct evidence of that learning.

Clearly class teachers can, and regularly do, monitor the learning that goes on in their classrooms. Subject leaders could rely on self-monitoring by their colleagues and in the reality of most schools this will be a major source of evidence. However, we will concentrate on ways in which a subject leader can be more directly involved in developing a whole school picture. First, we need to look at what criteria subject leaders can use to help them decide what evidence to collect, where to find it and how to judge such evidence. There are numerous published sources of criteria that can be used to judge quality of learning. The Ofsted Handbook (Ofsted 1995a) offers general ones that inspectors use. Specific subject guidance is available in a separate publication (Ofsted 1996b) which provides inspectors with information about collecting and using evidence of learning and teaching in each subject. It builds on the earlier Ofsted handbook (1993) which identified criteria in all National Curriculum subject areas. For example, the identified criteria for design and technology indicate that quality learning is taking place when pupils:

- consistently use and extend their knowledge, understanding and skills as they design and make products;
- show curiosity in the investigation of properties of different materials;
- use an increasing range of techniques, processes and resources;
- show creativity in designing to meet particular needs;
- show perseverance in organizing, planning and making products;
- are evaluating at each stage of their work;
- are testing fairly against objective criteria;
- work independently or as part of a team.

These criteria form a useful basis for subject leaders constructing their own lists, as we can see in Case Study 12.1.

Other sources of such criteria are available in subject-specific literature and publications from subject associations. Another means of producing such criteria is to use a staff meeting to generate them in collaboration with colleagues. Such a list would have the advantages of being 'owned' by colleagues and more likely to be appropriate to the specific context of the school and the pupils in it. It is best to avoid being overambitious about such criteria with colleagues – start with a core list which everyone can endorse and considers achievable and then extend it based on the developing confidence and competence of colleagues.

Monitoring can be carried out whenever subject leaders have the opportunity to be in colleagues' classrooms. Observations, team-teaching and class swaps all have the potential for collecting valuable evidence of pupils' learning. Visits set up exclusively for monitoring can be more threatening to colleagues and need to be approached sensitively, emphasizing the collaborative aspects and the benefits to both teacher and subject leader of the

Case Study 12.1 Monitoring learning

A group of design and technology subject leaders, working together at a cluster meeting, set about identifying a set of criteria which they could use to monitor learning in their schools, with the intention of sharing examples of practice with each other, in order to develop their competence in recognizing and recording quality learning. They brainstormed, without reference to the Ofsted criteria, their own ideas about what 'quality' learning might involve. Their list was extensive. They then compared their criteria with the Ofsted set and through discussion refined their ideas to produce a commonly agreed list. They used this to monitor work in a selected class in their own schools (based on classroom observations, carried out with the support of all the head teachers involved in the cluster initiative) and the group used a follow-up meeting to share their findings and further refine their list.

experience. The professional dialogue about the subject and how pupils learn, based on evidence collected during a visit can be a valuable learning experience for both parties. This is especially the case when subject leaders are observing colleagues working with children of different ages or phases from those they teach themselves. In this situation subject leaders might initiate the session on this basis – 'I would like to find out more about Y2 because I have not taught that age group, would you mind if I spent a session with you?' Observation visits work best in schools where a genuine collaborative culture (see Chapter 13) exists and where head teacher and senior managers are supportive. If every subject leader has, at some time, the opportunity to monitor one or more colleagues in this way, it is less threatening for all; it becomes a part of 'the way we do things around here'. If head teachers are doing classroom observations (however informally), the subject leaders should be discussing criteria of quality learning with them and being provided with feedback by the head teachers of what evidence they have seen. Similarly, subject leaders may find discussions with other adults who spend time in the classrooms productive. This might be an LEA adviser, a tutor from higher education or a student on block school experience. Regular meetings with parent helpers or classroom assistants (perhaps set up to help them identify ways they can support learning) and with groups of children to talk about their work can provide another more informal, but sometimes revealing, source of information about learning. Organizing class swaps requires no extra resourcing, but does provide excellent opportunities to gain real insights into pupils' learning, as Case Study 12.2 illustrates.

In situations where classroom observations are not yet established or considered too difficult to organize because of resourcing, subject leaders need to find other ways of gaining access to pupils' learning. Suggestions in Chapter 3 included sampling/moderating assessments of pupils' work (either by the

Case Study 12.2 A class swap

Sarah and Frank are respectively the science and mathematics subject leaders in a 10-teacher primary school. Sarah has a Year 2 class and Frank a Year 5 class. With their head teacher's support they have organized a class swap at the end of each half term. The schemes of work in the school are based on units of work which last for half a term. They agreed to collaboratively plan lessons at the end of each unit that could be used as a means of reviewing with the classes what they have learnt (in the respective subjects) and explore the application of the pupils' learning in new contexts.

For example, just before Christmas, the lesson Sarah took with Frank's class was based on the work they had done on electric circuits. She organized a discussion and quiz with them before challenging them to make Christmas cards with working circuits attached to them. Sarah's class had been working on addition and subtraction with money and Frank's lesson included buying Christmas presents for family members with fixed sums of pocket money.

After the swap lesson the head teacher provided both with an opportunity to meet for 30 minutes to discuss what they found out. At that time the head teacher took both classes for a reading session – the older children reading a story to a younger one (in pairs) and then listening to the younger ones read from their reading books.

To date, both Sarah and Frank have reported the value of the initiative and the valuable insights it is providing them both into the learning of their subjects in the school. The head teacher hopes to extend the approach to other subject areas.

subject leader alone, or, more usefully, at meetings with groups of colleagues or a whole staff) and encouraging colleagues to send pupils to see subject leaders regularly with interesting examples of what they have done (about which the subject leaders can talk to them, as well as seeing the outcomes). Other approaches could involve passing a camera around colleagues and asking them to photograph children's work (in, say, art) or a tape-recorder (for music). The value of subject leaders regularly looking at pupils' work from other classes, across year groups and key stages, should not be underestimated. The Ofsted *Framework* (Ofsted 1995a) places emphasis on 'progress', in lessons and across units of work, a term, a year and over a pupil's school career. This needs to inform the samples of work subject leaders monitor – for example, a portfolio of individual children's work over a term will enable judgements about progress to be made.

The other main source of data for subject leaders concerning quality of learning is likely to come from the informal and formal assessment and recording procedures, such as those referred to in Chapter 6, that are used in the school. This data will help inform judgements about pupils' progress over time. In some subjects, of course, SAT results will be a significant measure of pupils' achievements, but it would be disappointing to think that was the only indicator a subject leader chose to use – even if it is, in some quarters, the main measure of success. Chapter 6 has already addressed issues related to SAT results, comparison with other schools and value-added issues. Ofsted (1995a: section 4.1) makes judgements about the extent to which:

- the attainment of pupils at age 7 and 11 meets or exceeds national standards, particularly in English, mathematics and science;
- high, average and low attaining pupils, including those with special educational needs, progress as well as or better than expected;
- the attainment and progress of minority groups of pupils is comparable with others in the school;
- the school sustains high levels of attainment or is improving.

Task 12.1

Consider what evidence you currently have which allows you to make judgements related to pupils' attainment, such as those listed above. What could you do to obtain the evidence you need, if you identify gaps in what you already know?

The variety of record keeping systems in schools at the present time is considerable. Some are incredibly comprehensive (and sometimes unmanageable to maintain), others are so minimalist that they offer limited scope for providing monitoring data. A balance needs to be struck between practicality and the benefits to be gained from the evidence records can provide. Subject leaders should be contributing to discussions about these systems to ensure the needs of their subjects are met. Our preference is for holistic profiling approaches to record keeping, which enable schools to meet statutory requirements, but provide a rounded picture of the learner over the period they are in a school, identifying strengths and weaknesses as well as targets for future learning and evidence of those targets being met (Ritchie 1991).

Monitoring teaching

Much of the above applies to monitoring teaching, although the purposes and some of the strategies may be different. A key point to begin with is to remember that the monitoring of teaching is not done just for the sake of it – it should have a formative purpose which leads to improved teaching. It should help teachers understand the ways in which they can develop professionally. Monitoring of teaching has greater potential for contributing to school improvement than the monitoring of learning. It is, after all, changes to teachers' practice that will have the most likely impact on pupils' achievements (see Chapter 4). Those changes can be valuably informed by insights gained through monitoring. There are considerable links (in theory) between the monitoring of teachers' classroom work and the appraisal process. Teachers are having to become more used to others making judgements about their professional competence (new entrants to the profession will be even more familiar with these processes in the context of the new competences for newly qualified teachers and the way they are assessed; DfEE 1998a). Subject leaders can help establish a climate in which colleagues feel confident and comfortable to have others visit their classrooms and comment on what goes on. Indeed they may even learn to welcome it as an opportunity to celebrate their professional achievements.

Criteria for judging the quality of teaching will be significantly different, but linked, to those that apply to learning. The criteria in the Ofsted *Framework* (Ofsted 1995a: section 5.1) are generic and deal with the extent to which teachers:

- have a secure knowledge and understanding of the subjects or areas they teach;
- set high expectations so as to challenge pupils and deepen their knowledge and understanding;
- plan effectively;
- employ methods and organizational strategies which match curricular objectives and the needs of all pupils;
- manage pupils well and achieve high standards of discipline;
- use time and resources effectively;
- assess pupils' work thoroughly and constructively, and use assessments to inform teaching;
- use homework effectively to reinforce and/or extend what is learned in school.

Task 12.2

Produce a list of indicators of quality of teaching specific to your subject area. Do this with colleagues if possible. Consider what evidence you would look for to judge whether these criteria are being met by a teacher.

Lists such as these can be a useful means of colleagues self-monitoring their teaching. It should not be too difficult for subject leaders to get colleagues to identify specific examples of how they consider such criteria are met in their classroom, or to encourage them to identify which ones are not being well met and think about how things could be improved. Of course, there are some problems attached to relying on teachers' own accounts of practice. What teachers report and what actually goes on are not necessarily the same. There is a considerable literature dealing with teachers' 'espoused theories' (what they say they are doing) and 'theories-in-action' (what they do) which builds on the seminal work of Donald Schön (see Argyris and Schön 1978; Schön 1983). Observation by others will help expose these differences, about which colleagues may not even be consciously aware. Indeed, audiotaping a lesson may achieve the same objective – it certainly did for one of us (Ritchie 1993). We remind you here of the strategies we suggested in Chapter 8 for supporting colleagues in dealing with situations like this, where we find ourselves to be living contradictions.

At a different level, aspects of teaching can be monitored through scrutiny of teachers' plans and class records. These are often monitored by head teachers in primary schools and there is no need for duplication of effort. However, subject leaders may need to make a head teacher aware of aspects of the subject that need particular attention (for example, is Science 1 adequately addressed in teachers' plans?). Subject leaders will also need feedback from their head teachers, if that is how teaching of the subject is monitored. Monitoring of plans and intentions can provide the evidence. Subject leaders need to demonstrate that: statutory requirements regarding National Curriculum coverage are being met; that time allocations for subjects are appropriate; that there is equal access for all pupils; that continuity and progression is provided.

Chapter 3 introduced other strategies for collecting evidence of teaching quality from a variety of sources, some of which we discussed above in the context of monitoring learning. Another area that will need regular monitoring is teachers' professional development needs and activities. The latter is relatively easy to monitor through pro formas updated every term (or year). Subject leaders who follow our advice about helping colleagues identify needs and action plans (Chapter 8), will be generating the evidence needed for monitoring as part of the processes suggested. Some aspects of teaching and teachers' professional work, such as teaching style, teachers' confidence and subject expertise and knowledge, may not need regular monitoring, although these are aspects that a subject leader needs to know about, and therefore are aspects to be audited.

In these sections we have focused on two important elements of schools that subject leaders need to monitor: learning and teaching. There were other aspects of subjects which also need to be monitored, for example resources and efficient use of money. Each individual subject leader will have to make decisions about priorities. It is not possible to monitor all aspects of a subject systematically all of the time. However there needs to be processes in place to ensure it happens, and that what it's decided needs monitoring is monitored.

The formative purpose of monitoring means that it is subject leaders' responsibility to make sure the best use possible is made of monitoring to inform their subjects' development in the school. As we stressed in Chapter 3, when looking at how information gathered through an audit can be used to set targets and plan the steps needed to achieve those targets, monitoring is part of an evaluation and planning process aimed at facilitating school improvement. Monitoring is essential to subject development planning – it is the way that subject leaders find out what needs doing next to move the subject forward. Evaluation is a term that is used in many different ways in education (for example: a teacher evaluating her or his lesson; a pupil evaluating a model they made in design and technology; a school staff evaluating a new mathematics scheme). We are using it to describe a process of analysis and interpretation of information about an activity to enable judgements to be made about that activity. It involves key questions such as 'What have I found out?' and 'What issues are highlighted that need addressing?' It is from these questions that future plans can be formulated, and in this way, evaluation has formative outcomes. Chapter 3 dealt with the processes of long term development planning and shorter term action planning, which have been revisited at various points throughout this book and are integral to formative outcomes. On other occasions, the goal of evaluation will be more summative, seeking to answer the question 'Did we achieve what we set out to achieve?' In this context, the need for ongoing monitoring to provide information for Ofsted inspectors, amongst others, will be a theme we address in the latter part of this chapter.

The results of monitoring and evaluation, especially if they provide a positive picture of a subject, deserve disseminating wherever appropriate. For example, letting parents, governors, feeder schools, secondary colleagues and LEA advisers know how well you are doing may reap longer term benefits. The children themselves are another audience that could be given the results of evidence of their achievements, as a confidence boost or to encourage more effort. Finally, before we leave monitoring and evaluation, we would suggest that subject leaders should periodically review and evaluate the monitoring process that is being used: Is it successful and why? What has been learnt from the process? Could monitoring be done more efficiently? Have the results been shared with appropriate audiences in an appropriate way? Has monitoring and evaluation been used to improve learning for children?

A subject leader's file

Subject leaders inevitably collect a considerable amount of paperwork and need to be able to access, sometimes in a hurry, a whole variety of sources of information. Therefore we advocate use of a subject leader file. This will probably be a lever arch file in which is stored all of the necessary information and the various documents that have been produced. It can be a resource for subject leaders and their colleagues and is probably best kept in the staff room where it is accessible.

The organization of an individual file will need to be designed to meet that individual's needs. However, the following are our suggestions of what might be included in a file:

- job description;
- Teacher Training Agency (TTA) subject leader standards;
- self-evaluation of your competence against the standards (dated and regularly reviewed);
- policy statements;
- scheme of work (if not too bulky);
- other related policies and guidelines;
- health and safety information;
- subject development plans, targets, action plans, review and evaluation sheets;
- task action plans (kept in date order, with the current one at the front);
- inventory of resources (central and in classes), including software, TV programmes etc;
- diary of key activities, especially when non-contact time is provided;
- monitoring data and analysis – or index of where such data is available;
- notes of support offered to colleagues, including their action plans and evaluations;
- minutes or notes of meetings – with head teacher (including review meetings/appraisal, with evidence of your effectiveness being evaluated), other subject leaders, colleagues;
- lists of courses attended – subject leader and colleagues, with evaluation sheets;
- information re local networks, cluster meetings, links with other schools (including international projects);
- other information re external links: community, subject association, governors, Ofsted, LEA.

This is a tall order, given the pressures on teachers, and we are not suggesting that all elements are included immediately. However, such files can build into valuable tools that can enhance subject leaders' work, facilitate the monitoring of that work and provide ample material to help them through Ofsted inspections.

External inspection

External inspection of primary schools, currently through Ofsted, is a fact of life that will not go away. We would not want to challenge the need for teachers to be accountable, although we might take issue with the imposed processes by which inspections are conducted. However, in the context of this book, we are seeking to offer advice to subject leaders to ensure they are appropriately prepared for a visit and survive the experience. We are increasingly finding school staff who are recognizing that their Ofsted inspections have been genuinely formative experiences, providing opportunities to celebrate successes as well as producing externally validated analyses of how schools can improve. There are others, of course, for whom the experience is demoralizing and less constructive.

Apart from being observed in the classroom, which should provide an ideal opportunity to illustrate good practice in the subject, an important part of the inspection process for the subject leader will be the individual interview that he or she will have with an inspector. The following list covers the sorts of questions that subject leaders are likely to be asked in such interviews:

- What is being achieved in your subject? How do you know? What opportunities do you have for finding out? If you have curriculum management (non-contact) time how do you use it?
- What are the priorities for development in your subject? How do you contribute to the school development plan? Is there a subject development plan? Do you have an action plan?
- How was the subject's policy developed? Is it subject to review?
- How would you describe your current roles and responsibilities as a coordinator/subject leader? How were you appointed? Do you have subject expertise, or just personal interest in your subject? How was your job description arrived at? Is it published?
- Do you have responsibility for a budget? If so, how do you manage it? What are your priorities for spending at present? What is planned for the future? Are you clear about ordering procedures, budget management and budget monitoring? Have you audited resources recently? Are there any gaps in current resources?
- What in-service training have teachers recently received on the subject? Have you led, or are you planning to lead, any in-service training? How do you support your colleagues?
- Have non-teaching staff or parents received any support (training, workshops or talks)?
- Has in-service training had any significant impact on the standards of pupils' work?
- What in-service training have you received as a subject leader and what impact has it had?
- How do you assess and keep records of work covered, pupils' achievements and progress? How is this information reported to parents and others?
- Are there any specific arrangements to support pupils with special needs in your subject?
- Are there any developments in your subject about which you are particularly pleased? Are there any constraints on developments in your subject?

This is a daunting list and not every subject leader will be asked about all areas in any one inspection, although each subject leader in a school should get broadly the same questions. Preparing for an inspection is clearly desirable and, as the list indicates, a subject leader's file, that we suggested in the previous section, offers access to answers to most of the questions a subject leader might be asked. When preparing for inspection, a key strategy is to give careful thought to 'selling' the subject and teachers' achievements. It is important that subject leaders are clear, in advance, what evidence can be offered to substantiate what they intend to say. Samples of work need to be provided that should include such evidence (for example, how ICT is being used in the subject). This sample should include children's work that illustrates aspects of practice which the inspectors may not see in classrooms, because of the specific lessons going on at the time of the inspection. It makes the inspectors' job easier if subject leaders provide them with what they need to see to write a positive report. For example, subject leaders might think about how they can show that pupils with special educational needs (SEN) are supported – having a couple of specific examples from classes in Key Stages 1 and 2 to share (which will also allow them to talk about continuity through their schools). Some subject leaders practise the interview by getting a subject leader from another school (perhaps where there has been a recent inspection) to act as a 'critical friend' and role-play an interview.

Task 12.3

Consider the list of Ofsted questions and identify those that you would currently find difficult to answer. Decide what action is needed to enable you to provide a convincing response.

Many subject leaders have found it helpful to look at inspection reports from local schools (which are available on the Internet) or, of course, for their own schools if there were inspections prior to their arrival. This gives some ideas of issues that are being highlighted either currently, or historically in a particular school. Another source of such information is publications such as *Subjects and Standards* (Ofsted 1996a) which summarizes inspection findings. This report indicated key issues that many schools needed to face to remedy what the report called 'the current unsatisfactory situation' with regard to subject management. Those issues concerned how subject coordinators (*sic*) may:

- develop into managers for their subjects;
- have opportunities to influence policy and planning, to monitor and guide teaching, and to oversee resource provision for their subjects throughout the school;
- have and maintain, or in the case of non-specialists, acquire adequate specialist knowledge to make them effective and confident in their roles;
- have sufficient time to carry out these responsibilities;
- have access to the necessary in-service training and contacts, and opportunities to lead subject training for colleagues.

Most Ofsted inspections lead to the identification of issues that individual schools need to address through post-inspection action plans. Subject leaders, where the issue relates to their subjects, clearly have a key part to play in the production and implementation of these action plans. The planning process involved should not be too different from that discussed in Chapter 3, although the evidence of the need for action will be of a different type. Indeed, to develop an effective detailed action plan, subject leaders may need to supplement Ofsted findings with more detailed information from audits they subsequently conduct focused on the specific issue raised. Even if a report does not identify issues for a subject requiring immediate action, the post-Ofsted period may be an appropriate time for a subject leader to take stock of the subject's development using the evidence the inspection has provided.

Summary

This chapter has examined the contribution of monitoring and evaluation to the process of school improvement. It has highlighted different aspects of monitoring related to learning and teaching that need the attention of subject leaders (and their head teachers). Monitoring is a relatively new area of responsibility for many subject leaders and is one that needs approaching with sensitivity. Although the culture of most schools is changing and the ethos of schools is becoming more conducive to ongoing monitoring and evaluation, there remain schools and colleagues for whom such processes are threatening and not recognized as having professional benefit. It is our view that, whatever the origins of the need for more systematic monitoring and evaluation in schools, the value of these activities to school improvement is immense, and far outweigh the problems they present. Decisions about how to improve things for a subject can only be taken if we have an accurate picture of what is already going on, just as appropriate decisions about how to move children's learning forward need to be based on careful assessments of what they already think, know and can do.

The chapter has also offered advice about the contribution subject leaders can make to a school inspection by an external source, such as Ofsted. Again we have argued for this to be seen as a constructive process allowing subject leaders to celebrate successes and, where necessary, receive and deal constructively with evidence of aspects of a subject's delivery that needs improving.

13

MANAGEMENT OF CHANGE

Introduction

For the last decade teachers have experienced a period of rapid change which has often led to uncertainty and uneasiness. Some of the changes have been welcomed and have had a positive impact on the quality of teaching and learning. Others have been less popular and the impact of these would be argued by some to have been negative. To some extent we have 'grown too accustomed to seeing [teachers] oppressed by external changes' (Mortimore 1997:x). However change is not going to go away nor should it – change is the way we improve. We believe teachers can and should be the active prompters of change aimed at improving the quality of pupils' learning. The role of subject leaders as agents of change is an aspect of their work that is tackled in this chapter. Managing change is not always easy and can sometimes be a painful process. Supporting colleagues in managing changes has been addressed throughout the book. As agents of change, subject leaders need appropriate personal style, authority, support, a good track record and vision. Change can involve an individual at the classroom level or it can be whole school change involving every teacher.

The present discussion will address some general aspects of the process of change, beginning with a discussion about school cultures and the effect of these on improvements that a subject leader may be seeking to achieve. Change can be imposed from outside the institution or motivated by internal pressure. Some schools are more conducive to change than others and indicators of this will be outlined. There are likely to be constraints on change in any institution and subject leaders need to identify and minimize these factors. In tackling these, subject leaders will often find themselves in circumstances that involve conflict. The chapter will examine the implications of such situations. The final section will draw together themes related to school improvement and the contribution subject leaders can potentially make to this.

The culture of schools

Much has been written about the cultures of schools (Day *et al.* 1993; Whitaker 1993; West 1995). Cultures relate to 'how we do things around here' – they depend on: personalities; understandings, attitudes, meanings and norms; relationships; beliefs and values; symbols, rituals and ceremonies; preferred behaviours, styles and stances (based on Nias *et al.* 1989).

Task 13.1

Think about how things are in your school and what this says about the culture in which you work. Consider relationships (between adults, pupils and pupils/adults), leadership, traditions and customs, symbols evident around the school, management and organizational structures, and values (shared and individual). Consider the extent to which the culture of your school could be described as 'individualist' or 'collaborative'.

Fullan and Hargreaves (1992) identified a continuum of management cultures (Figure 13.1) that are frequently cited as a way of understanding the process of change in schools.

Clearly, the framework in Figure 13.1 is unlikely to match the reality of any particular school. Day *et al.* (1993) suggest each type is likely to be a continuum from strong to weak forms of each. However, it is helpful in identifying aspects of a school's approach that may be adapted to encourage a more collaborative approach, which is seen as most conducive to change and school improvement. Cultural life in a school is a constructed reality and leaders play a key part in building this reality (Sergiovanni and Corbally 1984). Cultures can be changed and, although the head teacher may be in the best position to encourage this, subject leaders can initiate and/or support those changes.

Another way of analysing school cultures is offered by Handy (1985) who refers to 'role', 'task', 'club' and 'person' cultures. The significance of role and task cultures is developed by West (1995, 1996) who identifies disadvantages of schools that operate exclusively within a role culture – individuals taking responsibility for specific functions in a hierarchical structure are not necessarily efficient and may reduce the responsibility and commitment others have for these functions. For example, if a science subject leader is working in a school where she is seen to be exclusively responsible for developing the science curriculum, she may find that her colleagues think they do not have to play a part in that development – it will be done for them. An alternative

Culture of separation →	Cultures of connection →	Culture of integration
	Balkanization Separate and competing groups First loyalty to group rather than the school (where these are different) Squabbles over resources/ spaces Poor continuity and expectations of pupils	
Individualism Mistakenly associated with professional autonomy Teachers teach largely within the isolated privacy of their classrooms Insulation from observation and criticism Reluctant to share professional problems Anti-intellectual suspicion of serious educational debate Discussion mainly concerned with gossip about the particularities of school life	**Comfortable collaboration** High participation in decision making Warmth, camaraderie on personal level Reactive, not proactive planning Collaboration at level of advice-giving, sharing materials Oral rather than written tradition of communication Little contact with theory, reflective practice or outside ideas	**Fully collaborative** Strong personal and professional relationships Commonly held social and moral intentions Failure and uncertainty not protected or defended but shared and discussed Individual and group simultaneously and inherently valued
	Contrived collegiality Sets of formal, bureaucratic procedures Attention to joint planning and consultation – but administratively imposed Principles of individual teacher judgement eroded	

Figure 13.1 Management cultures
Source: adapted from Day *et al*. 1993; Fullan and Hargreaves 1992

is for the subject leader to encourage a collaborative team approach within a task culture – groups work on specific tasks at specific times and responsibility for those tasks is shared. West (1996) advocated a mixed economy response, recognizing the value of designated roles for some aspects of school development and the use of task-teams for others. We would argue for subject leaders to play a significant part in task-teams related to their subject areas. The key message is that subject leaders cannot, nor should they be expected to, do it alone.

The nature of change as a process

Change is an ongoing process and not an event. According to Fullan (1991:117), 'educational change depends on what teachers do and think – it is as simple and as complex as that'. Much has been written about managing change in educational settings, drawing on lessons that can be learnt from looking at change in other organizations (e.g. Eason 1985; Fullan 1991; Whitaker 1993). In schools, change or innovation can be initiated externally (nationally or locally) or internally (individual, senior manager or whole school). It can be imposed or voluntary, statutory or non-statutory, welcome or unwelcome and have a positive or negative effect. The origins of a change and its nature will clearly affect teachers' responses and subject leaders' approaches to managing it. Although externally imposed change, for example the implementation of a post-Ofsted action plan, can be the least popular and the most threatening, it can also, on occasions, provide a useful 'stick' or 'wedge' that a subject leader can use to move the school forward in a positive direction. Some externally imposed changes, which are considered to be negative in their impact on school life, may need to be adapted to ensure they are congruent with colleagues' values and aspirations. As Hopkins *et al.* (1994:14) remind us, 'if reform initiatives are to succeed, they need to be reinvented in local settings'. Change and improvement are not necessarily synonymous. Managing change therefore, involves identifying needs, planning, implementing plans and evaluating the success of the change. Subject leaders should be facilitating each element of this process and looking for opportunities to delegate in order to give colleagues ownership of the change process. Consequently it is important for them to understand as much as possible about the nature of change. MacGilchrist *et al.* (1997) in their fascinating book *The Intelligent School* offer some key messages about change:

- it takes time;
- a school's capacity for change will vary;
- change is complex;
- change needs to be well led and managed;
- teachers need to be the main agents of change;
- pupils need to be the main focus of change.

Fullan (1991) claims that change in schools can take place simultaneously through: the introduction of new equipment and materials (a new reading scheme); the introduction of new behaviours and practices (paired reading activities); or through the introduction of new beliefs and attitudes (a different approach to the teaching of reading). He provides (Fullan 1991:105–7) a much quoted set of assumptions about change which remain as significant now as when they were first postulated. These can be summarized as follows:

- Don't assume that your ideas about changes are the ones that ought to be implemented.
- Assume that individuals who are attempting to implement changes will continually need clarification about them in order to make sense.
- Assume that successful change will inevitably involve some conflict and disagreement.
- Assume that people will only change if there is pressure to do so, a supportive environment, and opportunities to share experiences with others in similar situations.
- Assume that it will take two or three years for significant change to take place.
- Don't assume that the change itself has been rejected if it fails to be implemented – there may be other factors which have contributed to the failure.
- Assume that it is impossible to bring about widespread change in a school: aim to increase the number of people affected.
- Assume that you need a knowledge of the factors that affect change and draw up a plan that takes account of them and the above assumptions.
- Don't assume that knowledge can be the sole basis for decisions. They will usually be based on a combination of knowledge, politics and intuition.
- Assume that change will be fraught with problems and new challenges.

On a lighter note, Murphy's laws regarding change are worth considering:

- if any thing can go wrong, it will;
- nothing is as simple as it seems;
- everything takes longer than you expect;
- if you try to please everybody, someone is not going to like it;
- whatever you want to do, you have to do something else first;
- it is easier to get into something than out of it;
- if you explain something so clearly that no one can misunderstand, someone will.

When initiating or planning change it is vital to analyse the constraints that might exist. These can be grouped in the following way:

1 nature of change – origins, purpose, realistic, ownership, reward (for self and others);
2 resources – human, financial, time, physical;
3 human – personalities, skills, knowledge and understanding, professionalism, professional skills, motivation;

4 institutional – management structures, timing, history, culture;
5 external – policy, parental pressures/responses.

In Chapter 3, the use of force field analysis was advocated as a means of minimizing inhibiting (or resisting) forces and maximizing driving ones. Clearly such an analysis is helpful in any situation where a change is being implemented.

Schools have multiple goals and frequently face multiple changes. School development planning, as discussed in earlier chapters, is an important means of prioritizing within such a context. In the 1990s, the externally imposed changes have tended to focus on structures of schooling and the content of the curriculum (Whitaker 1993) rather than on learning and cultures. It is our contention that the time has come for a greater emphasis on teaching and learning and hence for a major role for subject leaders in supporting colleagues in making improvements in these areas. Change is likely to involve an interplay between personal, interpersonal and curriculum dimensions (Eason 1985). Additionally, we would want to advocate a gradual, 'small step' approach to change rather than one that involves schools or individuals taking a big leap into the unknown.

Ferguson (1982) offered a framework concerning individuals' approaches to change, emphasizing the different ways in which teachers might deal with change at a personal level:

1 change by exception – what I have always believed is right, this exception proves the rule;
2 incremental change – I was almost right before but now I am;
3 pendulum change – I was wrong before, but now I'm right;
4 paradigm change – I was partially right before, now I'm a bit more partially right.

The last response is the most constructive as it sees change as a journey that is ongoing throughout a professional's working life. The other responses have inherent problems that are likely to have adverse effects on the long term impact of the change on the quality of pupils' learning. Schools that are receptive to change are often those which have a previous history of change, have strong staff commitment, high morale and a willingness to invest extra effort. Changes that work are likely to be seen as relevant to teachers in that they will meet an individual need and offer them and their pupils significant benefits.

Task 13.2

Consider changes that have been implemented in your school over the last year. Which have been most successful and why? Do you consider your school conducive to change? Analyse the factors that are significant in your particular school setting. If improvements are necessary, what could you do to support your colleagues in making them more receptive to change?

Change in schools and professional development or learning are inextricably linked. Garratt (1987) analysed schools as learning organizations and postulated the need for

$L \geq C$ (where L is the learning involved and C the rate of change).

Unfortunately, the reality of the last few years in schools has been

$C > L$

The rate of change has outstripped the professional learning needed to cope with it. It is partly the responsibility of subject leaders to ensure colleagues' professional development and learning is sufficient for them to cope with the changes being implemented. This reinforces that a learning school is one where everyone, teacher and pupil, is constantly learning. Indeed Barth (1990) suggested that a head teacher should be the head learner as well. Subject leaders should be setting examples for colleagues through their own willingness to continue to learn.

Conflict and dealing with it

Primary school staff rooms are environments where, on the whole, conflict is avoided at all costs. Controversial topics may be ignored and differences of opinion about professional issues minimized. The need to get on together in a small staff often overrides other considerations. Subject leaders may have to handle numerous potential sources of conflict in schools: conflict with colleagues, between colleagues, with the head, with governors, with external agencies (including inspectors), with parents and with children. Some of these will be personal, others professional. While some conflict is best avoided, in other situations, such as managing change, dealing with conflict constructively can be a way forward.

To help with this, it is necessary to analyse the potential origins of conflict. These may be related to gender, power, belief systems, cultural differences, age, management structures or personalities. Teachers are well aware of the need to avoid conflict situations with children and parents by anticipating problems and defusing situations that arise, perhaps by postponing a discussion, involving another colleague or distracting the individual with another activity or focus. In contexts where colleagues or other professionals are the source of the conflict such strategies will not necessarily be the most effective. Conflicts that arise through bigotry, sexism, racism or because of personality reasons are beyond the scope of this treatment, although we would, in passing, advocate the need to expose such conflict to others and challenge it. We are more interested in conflict that may arise in the context of encouraging or supporting changes. Some of these situations can be dealt with through a more careful explanation and discussion of the issues.

Change in schools is often ineffective because staffs create illusions of effectiveness – teachers convince each other they are already doing a good job and all that is required of them. However, in a staff discussion about a new initiative, the colleague who says what others may be thinking, but keeping quiet about, provides the opportunity for issues to be aired openly, clarified and jointly resolved. This is a situation where 'conflict' can be constructive. Dealing with differences of opinion frankly and in a context of mutual respect is a way of moving everyone forward. One of the difficulties of dealing with issues like this in primary schools is the extent to which teachers see their professional work as inextricably linked to them as human beings. In industry, it is possible to criticize the way a colleague does a job without it being taken as a criticism of that person as a whole. Teachers tend not to react in this way – criticisms of their work are criticisms that are taken very personally. Subject leaders can help by being self-critical, open and encouraging others to provide constructive criticism of their own work and reacting to it in a professional way. Barth (1990) distinguishes 'congeniality' from 'collegiality' and stresses the increased potential of schools where the latter is valued above the former. He claims (1990:31): 'Decisions tend to be better. Implementation of decisions is better. There is a higher level of trust and morale amongst adults. Adult learning is energized and more likely to be sustained.'

Clearly there may be some entrenched 'blockers' amongst staffs who will be very difficult, if not impossible, to move forward. However, when individuals resist change they are not usually working in active opposition, but demonstrating a threat to their security (Whitaker 1993). 'It isn't that people resist change as much as they don't know how to cope with it' (Fullan 1991:xiv). Subject leaders need to accept this as natural and, to some extent, inevitable. They should listen to what is being expressed and try and understand the threat that their colleagues perceive. The fact that professionals have feelings about change needs acknowledging – subject leaders should be caring and concerned for their colleagues and act as an ally, not an opponent. In some cases subject leaders may need to help colleagues protect what is perceived to be under threat while moving them forward. Change can undermine teachers' confidence and belief in their competence. In Chapter 8, a 'health warning' was offered about the danger of exposing colleagues' weaknesses – turning them from unconscious incompetents to conscious incompetents, from content to dissatisfied professionals. Such a stage may be necessary, but should be handled sensitively and in the context of offering support for colleagues to become conscious competents. Whitaker (1993) suggests that teachers go through phases of shock, withdrawal, acknowledgement and adaptation when dealing with change. They will need different kinds of support at different stages. The use of SWOT analysis, which encourages teachers to identify Strengths, Weakness, Opportunities and Threats related to a proposed change, can be an excellent strategy for exposing colleagues' feelings so that they can be openly discussed.

Roles of the subject leader in dealing with change

In supporting and managing change, subject leaders will need to be an initiator, mediator (especially where external forces for change are involved), facilitator, planner, manager (of resources and people), problem solver, adviser, participant, monitor, evaluator, collaborator and leader (of a team or whole staff). Those are a lot of different hats to wear (especially when worn at the same time as maintaining a full time teaching responsibility) and clearly some subject leaders will favour some of these roles above others. Communicating is essential to managing change – colleagues need to be kept informed of purposes, approaches and how things are going. The most effective leadership strategy for managing change is probably encouraging collaboration and delegation – giving colleagues ownership of the change and helping them overcome difficulties together. Colleagues need to be empowered to make changes. As Elliot (1977) said, 'the best way to improve practice lies not so much in trying to control people's behaviour as in helping them control their own by being more aware of what they are doing'. An agent of change needs to be constantly alert to what is happening as changes are implemented – listening to what colleagues are saying, encouraging reflection and review and providing regular feedback. Motivation is essential if colleagues are going to invest time and effort in making changes. This will be helped if they feel that they are heard, noticed, encouraged, trusted, appreciated and valued, informed, helped to clarify ideas, helped to develop skills and comptences, challenged and extended. Case Study 13.1 illustrates one subject leader's role in bringing about change.

School improvement

'School improvement is a distinct approach to educational change that enhances student outcomes as well as strengthening the school's capacity for managing change' according to Hopkins *et al.* (1994:3). We have already recognized in this chapter that not all change is improvement, but all improvement involves change. The literature relating to school improvement is even more extensive than that relating to educational change (Ainscow *et al.* 1994; Hopkins *et al.* 1994; Hargreaves 1995; Reynolds *et al.* 1996). Much of this literature seeks to link school effectiveness (what characteristics define an effective school) with school improvement (the process by which schools change). Subject leaders need to be aware of the first and engaged in the second. Sammons *et al.* (1995:8) offer a concise summary of characteristics found in effective schools. These are:

- professional leadership;
- shared vision and goals;
- a conducive learning environment;
- concentration on teaching and learning;

Case Study 13.1 Managing change

Jane was appointed to her school as a newly qualified teacher (NQT) with responsibility for physical education (PE) (her specialism) about two years ago. The school had a new head teacher, no policy for PE and was in a period of rapid change that was being resisted by many of the long established staff. Jane soon found out that no one really liked teaching PE, because 'they couldn't do it' and felt threatened by having 'an expert' brought in.

In her first term Jane realized that much of the equipment needed attention, with some being dangerous, and that the storage facilities did not meet health and safety standards. Jane checked the legal requirements and discussed the situation with the head teacher and some of the more open members of staff who agreed with her that something needed to be done. Jane therefore set about planning how she could bring the equipment and its storage in line with the legal requirements but at the same time improve the teaching of PE. She arranged for a visit from the LEA adviser and a health and safety officer and persuaded the head teacher to replace some of the old equipment and asked the parent association to help provide suitable storage boxes and stands. She talked informally with her colleagues about the problems and tested their reactions to the changes that she needed to make to where the equipment was to be stored in future. Several staff did not like what was happening but Jane was able to point out that there was very little choice.

As the new equipment started to arrive Jane spent some time explaining how to use it and establishing routines for putting it away. During one of these sessions one of her colleagues wanted to know how Jane would use some of the equipment with her class. Jane agreed to do a demonstration at lunchtime for anyone who wanted to come that went very well so, following a discussion with the head teacher, she asked for volunteers to look at the scheme of work. Although it hasn't always been easy, Jane has steadily worked through each part of the scheme with her colleagues and has been able to revise it completely. With one exception, who is about to retire anyway, all the staff feel happier teaching PE, like the scheme and now approach Jane for advice.

- purposeful teaching;
- high expectations;
- positive reinforcement;
- monitoring progress;
- pupil rights and responsibilities;
- home–school partnerships;
- a learning organization.

Clearly these characteristics have a resonance, as you would expect, with much that has been advocated in this book.

Task 13. 3

Which of the characteristics from Sammons *et al.* (1995) do you consider to be evident in your school? Which of those that you consider to be less well addressed do you consider that you as a subject leader could influence? How?

Involvement in school improvement as a process of change has also been an ongoing theme of this book. The metaphor of a journey, introduced in the discussion above about educational change, is one often used for school improvement – it is the journey of a school seeking to improve the quality of the educational experience of its pupils. Subject leaders may not be the captain of the ship, but they have a key function, perhaps equivalent to the mate. Improvement is a dynamic process that should lead to a school moving forward towards a situation of improved effectiveness or a greater degree of success in their core function – pupils' learning. Hopkins *et al.* (1994) provide a model (Figure 13.2) to analyse schools' success at journeying. In the same book, Hopkins *et al.* identify 'doors to school improvement' which include:

- collegiality;
- making use of research findings;
- action research;
- curriculum initiatives;
- teaching strategies;
- self-managing school;
- school development planning.

These are, again, themes we have sought to develop throughout this book. We have encouraged subject leaders to foster collaborative approaches based on collegiality; we have offered insights from research and literature to support subject leaders in their work; we have focused on the potential of action

Process \ Outcomes	Ineffective	Effective
Dynamic	Wandering	Moving
Static	Stuck	Promenading

Figure 13.2 Four expressions of school cultures in the context of school improvement

Source: from Hopkins *et al.* 1994

research as a tool for professional development and change; we have emphasized the need for subject leaders to focus on teaching strategies as well as more mundane maintenance and management tasks; we have explored the importance of whole school development and planning in which all teachers are actively involved.

Task 13.4

Reflect on your own school situation. Which of the above conditions most appropriately describes the situation of your school in the context of your subject's development? If your school is not yet 'moving', how could you contribute to ensuring it does?

Summary

To be an effective agent of change, subject leaders need to understand the nature of change and the processes it can involve. This chapter has sought to provide insights into this aspect of subject leaders' work. Change will have an impact on all teachers. Consequently, one of the changes that many subject leaders will need to facilitate in the next few years relates to this new approach to subject leadership – supporting colleagues in understanding the nature of the leadership dimensions and how they differ from more traditional approaches to coordination. Only when these changes become embedded in the culture of schools will subject leaders become truly effective and provide the support colleagues need.

14

PULLING IT ALL TOGETHER

Introduction

Leadership is not about one individual doing everything. It is about making things happen through working together and developing teams in which everyone has the potential to lead. Barth (1988) refers to 'a community of leaders', which very effectively sums up the situation in primary schools in which everyone has leadership responsibilities (e.g. as head teacher, deputy head teacher, subject leaders and class teachers) yet at the same time are members of a team in which they have individual responsibilities. While this can lead to conflicts of interest, it also has the potential for helping primary schools to be organizations that are strong enough and flexible enough to manage the changes that will be required as they move into the next century. The allocation of responsibilities provides a basis for ensuring that the maintenance tasks are completed but the acceptance that everyone has different roles in different situations means that development tasks can be carried out quickly and imaginatively without the restrictions of a fixed hierarchy. How successful schools are in the future will depend on how effectively they can integrate these two ingredients into the organization.

Developing the whole school approach

The rapid changes that have taken place since 1989 in primary schools have, ironically, encouraged the development of whole school approaches to many aspects of school life. The need to respond to the introduction of, and changes to, the National Curriculum and to work towards meeting the requirements of Ofsted inspections, amongst other things, have combined to help 'break down the private individualist culture of primary schools and replace it with one characterized by openness, trust and cooperation' (Webb and Vulliamy 1996:158). Thus there is greater involvement of all staff in a wide range of tasks such as: the formulation of school development plans, the planning and policy making for implementing the National Curriculum, the compilation of school assessment portfolios, the planning and delivery of school-based INSET and the preparation for inspections. Another significant effect, of particular interest to us, is the increased recognition and acceptance of the part played by subject leaders in the management of the school.

Webb and Vulliamy (1996) also found that, in contrast, there are strong forces that are undermining the moves towards such cooperation continuing. We have also observed these trends. The allocation of separate roles and responsibilities to members of staff in general, and to subject leaders in particular, along with the increased workloads placed on them have resulted in much of the management work being done 'at home', in isolation, with little involvement of colleagues (Bell 1997). Such trends should be resisted and we have argued throughout this book that subject leaders, in particular, should not work in isolation. Rather they need to work closely with their colleagues and others to get things done, through collaboration and cooperation, based on an understanding of achieving shared goals, positive attitudes and respect for the contributions of others.

Recognizing contributions

The success, or otherwise, of subject leaders clearly depends, in part, on subject leaders themselves but it also depends on the head teacher and their colleagues. It is worth stopping to consider, therefore the contributions that each of these parties makes first to the leadership, management, development and delivery of the subject within the school and, second (see the next section), to the effectiveness with which subject leaders are able to do their job. Table 14.1 (based on Underwood 1996) shows the different contributions that the head teacher, subject leader and individual teachers make to the former. The important point is that everyone in the school has parts to play and a shared responsibility for the learning opportunities and teaching in the subject.

Supporting subject leaders

The effectiveness with which subject leaders do their job and the impact it has depends very much on the support they receive from both the head teacher and their colleagues.

Table 14.1 Contributions to the leadership, management, development and delivery of subjects

Head teachers should:
- encourage a shared ownership of the subject as an important element in children's learning and teaching in the school;
- encourage an overall sense of responsibility for the subject within which roles and specific responsibilities are clear;
- encourage the development of links with other schools and support agencies;
- show a positive attitude towards the subject;
- support the subject leader and enable him/her to provide clear leadership in the subject.

Subject leaders should:
- provide clear leadership in the subject;
- promote the subject as an important element of the curriculum, ensuring that all the requirements of the National Curriculum are met;
- work with colleagues to maintain links across the curriculum as a whole to ensure continuity and coherence of children's learning;
- support and encourage colleagues in their teaching and use of the subject;
- manage the provision and deployment of resources;
- monitor and evaluate the teaching, learning and development of the subject.

Individual teachers should:
(a) as another subject leader,
- identify links with the other subject and work to strengthen them establishing continuity and coherence in children's learning;
- be aware of ways in which the subject complements theirs and vice versa;

(b) as class teacher,
- contribute to the development of a policy and scheme of work for the subject and use these as the basis for their own short term plans;
- provide the best possible opportunities for children's learning in the subject and work towards improving their teaching and approach to the subject;
- work with the subject leader to monitor, record and evaluate children's progress and achievements;
- provide feedback to the subject leader on topics, teaching approaches, and resources for the subject;
- share successes and failures in order to encourage and support colleagues, helping to develop a shared responsibility for learning, teaching, management and leadership in the subject.

Source: based on Underwood 1996

Head teachers

Let us not forget that many head teachers have had to respond to the rapid changes of the 1990s and find themselves in positions that they could not have anticipated. Thus they have had to learn quickly a variety of skills and

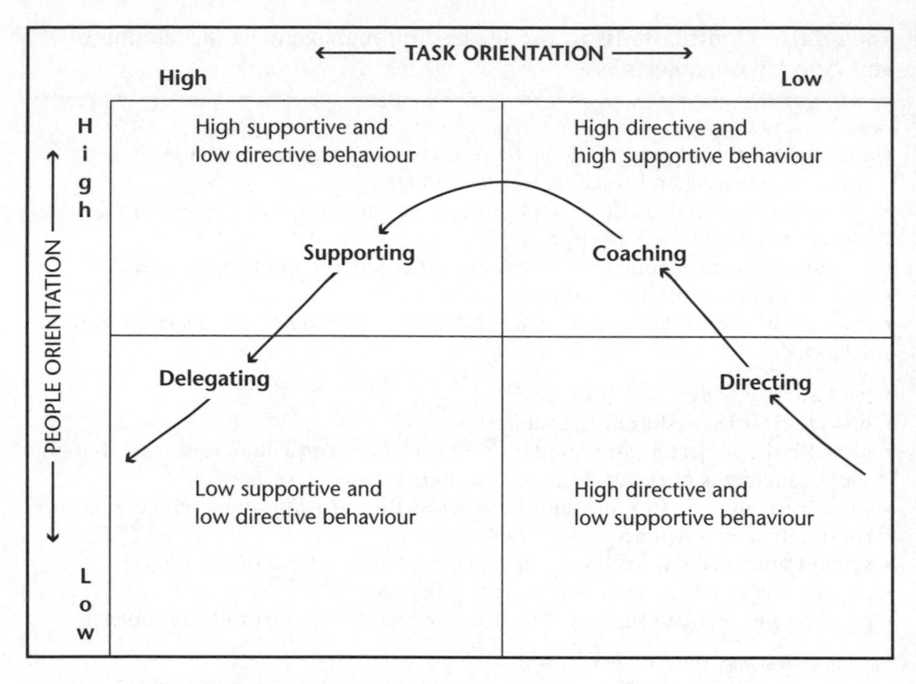

Figure 14.1 The situational leadership model
Source: redrawn from Blanchard *et al.* 1992

knowledge not previously required. In addition, the emphasis of their jobs has changed, often taking them away from management of the curriculum and towards other areas such as financial management. Of particular relevance to our discussion has been the need for head teachers to find ways of managing their staff as subject leaders as well as class teachers. This is not easy and often leads to frustration for both head teachers and subject leaders. Tensions often arise not necessarily because of different perceptions of the what a subject leader should do in theory but because of differences in priorities and what was wanted in practice (Bell 1990, 1992). Therefore, as we discussed in Chapter 7, it is important that head teachers spend time with their subject leaders and clarify the priorities and agree what is to be done.

Head teachers, however, need to take this a step further and make judgements about how best to support individual subject leaders. There are so many variables in every situation that in turn determine the type of support that is most appropriate. Skelton (1996), writing as an experienced head teacher, recognized that it takes time and additional training for head teachers to see the need to change the way in which they work with their own staff in order to support them in their different roles. He goes on to show how the 'situational leadership model' (Blanchard *et al.* 1992) can help. This model (Figure 14.1) acknowledges the maturity of the team member (in this case the subject leader as a member of the school team) and shows how the leadership style might change accordingly. Thus for a new and inexperienced subject leader the head teacher may provide strong direction, giving detailed instructions on how to do things. As the subject leader gains experience, or with more experienced people, the head teacher reduces the direction and increases the support to act first as coach then supporter. Finally both direction and support are reduced to a point where the subject leader has full delegation for their area of responsibility. Adopting such an approach will help head teachers: support subject leaders in a way that meets their needs; provide support and encouragement without smothering initiative; and advise but allow subject leaders to put their personality into the job. Most importantly head teachers will show that they value the work of their subject leaders. The ability, vision and confidence of head teachers to allow subject leaders to develop their own style and implement it is essential. Subject leaders in turn should learn from this approach not only in the way they lead their teams but also in the way they relate to their head teachers.

Class teachers

We have repeatedly made the important distinction that subject leaders work with their colleagues in two different contexts, one as other subject leaders and one as class teachers. In both situations the support and encouragement of their colleagues is essential if subject leaders are to be effective. The first requirement is that everyone remembers they are all subject leaders and are all class teachers thus experiencing many, if not all, of the same problems. An atmosphere of mutual support is therefore much more conducive to progress and success than one of antagonism and outright competition. Thus we cannot stress too strongly the need for cooperation and collaborative forms of working.

Everyone is working in teams within teams towards common goals and as such share responsibility for making progress in all areas, which puts the onus on everyone, as class teachers and subject leaders for other areas of the curriculum, to:

- talk with the subject leader to clarify the goals that have been set and to work towards them;
- contribute to tasks and discussions in a constructive manner;
- be clear about individual needs and the type of support that would be most useful;
- discuss issues with the subject leader rather than complaining behind his or her back;
- respond to consultations promptly and positively, presenting alternatives for consideration when appropriate;
- remember the subject leader cannot be expected to do everything.

A final reflection

There is no question that the post of subject leader in primary schools is a complex and demanding one that is developing rapidly. The National Standards for Subject Leaders (TTA 1998a) set out what is expected of subject leaders and define the core purpose 'to provide professional leadership and management for a subject to secure high quality teaching, effective use of resources and improved standards of learning and achievement for all pupils'. Thus subject leaders have a responsibility to the pupils in their school, the teachers with whom they work, parents, head teachers and other senior managers (including governors) and others in the school and the community. In order to meet these responsibilities subject leaders need to draw on a range of professional knowledge and understanding which is part subject-specific and part generic, to employ a range of skills (leadership, decision making, communication, self-management) and to draw on personal attributes (such as flexibility, energy, self-confidence, enthusiasm, intellectual ability, reliability, integrity and commitment; TTA 1998a).

In this book we have addressed the needs of subject leaders in primary schools as they work towards becoming more effective in the key areas (strategic direction and development of the subject; teaching and learning; leading and managing staff; and efficient and effective deployment of staff and resources) of subject leadership (TTA 1998a). The national standards set out the detail of what should be done but give no guidance as to how the job is to be done. We have attempted therefore to provide practical advice, supported by research, within a context of the wider issues related to curriculum development, school improvement, management and leadership in primary schools. In addition to the detailed treatment of each of the key areas we have identified several themes we would wish to emphasize as being essential to effective subject leadership. The first (emphasizing leadership) reflects the changing nature of the post, while the other three (bringing about children's learning; supporting professional development; and encouraging collegiality) provide the whole school context in which subject leaders need to operate if they are to have the influence they should.

Emphasizing leadership

The roles and responsibilities of subject leaders, as well as the terms used to describe those holding such posts, have evolved rapidly during the 1990s. More importantly the perceptions of the post have changed from a view that keeping the stock cupboard tidy was all that was required through the writing of policies and schemes of work to a recognition that issues of monitoring, evaluation and support for colleagues are also essential elements. Each of these stages were probably appropriate at the time and are important dimensions of being a subject leader. The current climate of change in education, however, requires a much greater emphasis on leadership. As we argued in Chapter 1 this has been a neglected dimension. As evidenced by the case studies and our research, subject leaders, however, are taking up this challenge and are starting to demonstrate their leadership skills by:

- sharing their vision for the subject as part of the whole curriculum through
- developing strong professional relationships with their head teacher, colleagues, children and others thereby
- empowering others to contribute and accept responsibility as members of a team that is
- working creatively to make decisions and meet the challenges involved in achieving the agreed goals.

Bringing about children's learning

We have stressed throughout the book that children's learning and the teaching necessary to bring this about should be at the centre of every school. Subject leaders clearly have a key role bringing about those high standards in teaching and learning in their subjects. By working with their colleagues in their classrooms to implement carefully drawn up policies and plans, subject leaders can improve the quality of the learning opportunities for the children. There are dangers, however, that individual subjects become seen as discrete entities so that the strength derived from the wholeness of the primary curriculum could be diminished. We would argue that the sum is greater than its parts and so encourage subject leaders to work together in a collaborative manner to establish a policy and the resulting practice for teaching and learning. Such an initiative will help to emphasize the approaches to teaching and learning that are valued and highlight the core purposes of the school. In so doing such a policy provides:

- a sound underpinning for all areas of the curriculum (not simply the National Curriculum) supporting continuity and coherence but not uniformity; and
- a basis for other activities such as planning, monitoring, evaluation and, in particular, staff development directly linked to classroom practice.

Supporting professional development

Everyone in a primary school is a teacher and a learner. No one is too old or too young to learn or to teach. Subject leaders are at the heart of these processes working to help and support their colleagues improve their knowledge, skills and understanding of both the subject and ways to teach and help children learn more effectively. At the same time subject leaders should be exploring, extending and reflecting on their own knowledge, skills and understanding in order to be more effective subject leaders. 'One of the most important developments in organization management over recent years has been the concept of *the learning organization*' (Day *et al.* 1998:19). If schools are to improve then it is vital that they are part of what might be called *the learning movement* in which learning takes place at both an individual and an organizational level. It is by working together that colleagues can learn from and teach each other in such a way that professional development is not about going on courses (although these can be very useful) but it is part of the school's culture, so that it (Day *et al.* 1998:18):

- 'fosters continuous professional learning';
- 'enables examples to be followed, feedback to be sought and received, and new skills to be supported';
- 'encourages [through collaborative work] the important learning processes of reflection and dialogue';
- integrates 'the professional learning objectives colleagues bring with them into a team task [so that they] become a vital part of the task itself.'

Encouraging collegiality

Schools are about people and as we have indicated throughout the book it is the strength of the relationships and the quality of the interactions which take place that are at the heart of their success (or failure). Despite all of the organizational changes since 1989 or before, primary schools have maintained the view that they teach children and that each child is seen as a complete individual. The increasing pressures and the risk of a fragmenting curriculum make it all the more difficult to hold onto this philosophy and resist it being broken down. The manner in which subject leaders approach their work could undermine the philosophy if they focus entirely on 'the subject' and allow themselves to become professionally isolated in carrying out their responsibilities. We would reinforce our arguments for subject leaders and their colleagues working together in a truly collaborative manner. Primary schools are complex organizations with many interlocking strands of activities, personalities, strengths and weaknesses. Each element has its discrete functions and effects but together they make up the organization that can only function effectively and successfully when:

- everyone has a shared understanding of what they are doing, what they are trying to achieve and how they are going to achieve it;
- teachers work together to improve and develop each other's practice;
- everyone has the potential to be a leader and the capability to be an agent of change;
- the structure of the organization is secure enough to deal with the day to day tasks but is flexible enough to respond quickly and positively to new challenges through the creativity and resourcefulness of its people.

As a final thought and to emphasize the importance of collegiality, we would like to conclude with the words attributed to the Chinese philosopher Lao Tse (531 BC):

> A leader is best when people barely know that he [*sic*] exists. Not so good when people obey and acclaim him. Worse when they despise him. Fail to honour people and they fail to honour you. But of a good leader who talks little, when his work is done, his aim fulfilled, they will say, 'we did it ourselves'.

APPENDIX

The following are some of the useful contacts that subject leaders may refer to for advice.

Association for Science Education
College Lane
Hatfield
Herts
AL10 9AA
01707 283000
www.ase.org.uk

Association of Teachers of Mathematics
7 Shaftesbury Street
Derby
DE23 8YB
01332 346599

British Association of Physical Training
6 Richmond Lodge
Victoria Avenue
Swanage
Dorset
BH19 1AN
01929 424030

Design and Technology Association
16 Wellesbourne House
Walton Road
Wellesbourne
Warwickshire
CV35 9JB
01789 470007
www.data.org.uk

Geographical Association
160 Solly Street
Sheffield
South Yorkshire
S1 4BF
0114 296 0088

Historical Association
59a Kennington Park Road
London
SE11 4JH
0171 735 3901
www.history.org.uk

Mathematical Association
259 London Road
Leicester
LE2 3BE
0116 270 3877
www.members.aol.com/mathsassoc/
mahomepage.html

Music Education Council
54 Elm Road
Hale
Altrincham
Cheshire
WA15 9QP
0161 928 3085

National Association for Design
Education
26 Dorchester Close
Mansfield
Notts
NG18 4QW
01623 631551

National Association for Environmental
Education
University of Wolverhampton
Walsall Campus
Gorway Road
Walsall
West Midlands
WS1 3BD
01922 631200

National Association for Primary
Education
NAPE National Office
University of Leicester
Barrack Road
Northampton
NN2 6AF
01604 36326
www.nape.org.uk

National Association for Special
Educational Needs
NASEN House
4–5 Amber Business Village
Amber Close
Amington
Tamworth
Staffordshire
B77 4RP
01827 311500
www.nasen.org.uk

National Association for the Teaching of
English
50 Broadfield Road
Broadfield Business Centre
Sheffield
South Yorkshire
S8 0XJ
0114 255 5419

National Grid for Learning
www.ngfl.gov.uk

National Society for Promoting Religious
Education
Church House
Great Smith Street
London
SW1P 3NZ
0171 222 1672

National Society for Education in Art
and Design
The Gatehouse
Corsham Court
Corsham
Wiltshire
SN13 0BZ
01249 714825

Physical Education Association of Great Britain and Northern Ireland
Suite 5
10 Churchill Square
Kings Hill
West Malling
Kent
ME19 4DU
01732 87588
www.teleschool.org.uk/pea

The Standards Site
www.standards.dfee.gov.uk

REFERENCES

Ainscow, M., Hopkins, D., Southworth, G. and West, M. (1994) *Creating the Conditions for School Improvement*. London: David Fulton.

Alexander, R. Rose, J. and Woodhead, C. (1992) *Curriculum Organisation and Classroom Practice in Primary Schools – A Discussion Paper*. London: DES.

Argyris, A. and Schön, D. (1978) *Organizational Learning*. Reading, MA: Addison-Wesley.

The Association for Science Education (ASE) (1981) *Science and Primary Education Paper No 3: A Post of Responsibility in Science*. Hatfield: ASE.

Avon LEA (1995) Planning for effective learning. Unpublished course materials for primary head teachers conference. Bristol.

Barth, R. (1988) Vision and school improvement, in F. W. Parkay (ed.) *Improving Schools for the Twenty-First Century*. Gainesville, FL: University of Florida.

Barth, R. (1990) *Improving Schools from Within*. San Francisco, CA: Jossey-Bass.

Bell, D. (1990) The role of science co-ordinators in primary schools in three local education authorities. Unpublished MEd thesis, University of Liverpool.

Bell, D. (1992) Co-ordinating science in primary schools: a Role model? *Evaluation and Research in Education*, 6(2,3): 155–71.

Bell, D. (1993) The role of the science co-ordinator, in R. Sherrington (ed.) *ASE Primary Science Teachers' Handbook*. Hemel Hempstead: Simon & Schuster.

Bell, D. (1996a) Subject specialist, co-ordinator, leader or manager? British Educational Research Association conference paper, Lancaster, September.

Bell, D. (ed.) (1996b) *Nuffield Primary Science: Science Co-ordinators' Handbook*. London: Collins Educational.

Bell, D. (1997) What do curriculum/subject co-ordinators in primary schools do?, British Educational Research Association conference paper, York, September.

Bell, D. (1998) Accessing science: challenges faced by teachers of children with learning difficulties in primary schools. *Support for Learning: British Journal of Learning Support*, 13(1): 26–31.

Bentley, D. and Watts, M. (1994) *Primary Science and Technology*. Buckingham: Open University Press.

Blanchard, K., Carew, D. and Parisi-Carew, E. (1992) *The One Minute Manager Builds High Performance Teams*. London: Harper Collins.
Blenkinsop, M. (1991) Curriculum co-ordination: formal and informal roles. *Management in Education*, 5(2): 2–3.
Board of Education (1905) *Suggestions for the Consideration of Teachers and Others concerned in the work of the Public Elementary Schools*, Command 2638. London: HMSO.
Bolam, R. (1982) Planning for a staff development policy. *British Journal of In-service Education*, 18: 14–17.
Campbell, R. J. (1985) *Developing the Primary School Curriculum*. London: Holt, Rhinehart and Winston.
Central Advisory Council for Education (England) (1967) *Children and their Primary Schools*, The Plowden Report. London: HMSO.
Coulby, D. and Ward, S. (1996) *Primary Core National Curriculum: Policy into Practice*. London: Cassell.
Cross, A. (1998) *Coordinating Design and Technology Across the Primary School*. London: Falmer Press.
Design and Technology Association (DATA) (1996) *The Design and Technology Primary Coordinator's File*. Wellesbourne: DATA.
Davies, J. (ed.) (1995) *Developing a Leadership Role in Key Stage 1 Curriculum*. London: Falmer Press.
Day, C., Hall, C., Gammage, P. and Coles, M. (1993) *Leadership and Curriculum in the Primary School*. London: Paul Chapman Publishing Ltd.
Day, C., Hall, C. and Whitaker, P. (1998) *Developing Leadership in Primary Schools*. London: Paul Chapman Publishing Ltd.
Department of Education and Science (DES) (1975) *A Language for Life*, The Bullock Report. London: HMSO.
Department of Education and Science (DES) (1978) *Primary Education in England: A survey by HMI*. London: HMSO.
Department of Education and Science (DES) (1982) *Mathematics Counts*, The Cockcroft Report. London: HMSO.
Department of Education and Science (DES) (1983) *Teaching Quality*, White Paper Command 8836. London: HMSO.
Department of Education and Science (DES) (1988) *School Teachers' Pay and Conditions Document 1988*. London: HMSO.
Department of Education and Science/Welsh Office (DES/WO) (1988) *National Curriculum: Task Group on Assessment and Testing*. London: HMSO.
Department for Education (DfE) (1994) *Code of Practice on the Identification and Assessment of Special Educational Needs*. London: HMSO.
Department for Education and Employment (DfEE) (1998a) *Teaching: High Status, High Standards – Requirements for Courses of Initial Teacher Training*, Circular 4/98. London: DfEE.
Department for Education and Employment (DfEE) (1998b) *The National Literacy Strategy: Framework for Teaching*. London: DfEE.
Department for Education and Employment (DfEE) (1998c) *Target Setting in Schools*, Circular 11/98. London: DfEE.
Department for Education and Employment (DfEE) (1998d) *Reducing the Bureaucratic Burden on Teachers*, Circular 2/98. London: DfEE.
Department for Education and Employment (DfEE) (1997) *From Targets to Action: Guidance to Support Effective Target Setting in Schools*. London: DfEE.

Eason, P. (1985) *Making School-centred INSET Work*. London: The Open University in association with Croom Helm.
Edwards, A. (1993) Curriculum co-ordination: a lost opportunity for primary school development? *School Organisation*, 13(1): 51–9.
Elliot, J. (1977) Conceptualising relationships between research/evaluation procedures and in-service education. *British Journal of In-service Education*, 4(2).
Ferguson, M. (1982) *The Aquarian Conspiracy*. London: Granada.
Fullan, M. (1991) *The New Meaning of Educational Change*, 2nd edn. London: Cassell.
Fullan, M. and Hargreaves, A. (1992) *What's Worth Fighting for in Your School?* Buckingham: Open University Press.
Galton, M. (1996) Teaching, learning and the co-ordinator, in J. O'Neill and N. Kitson (eds) *Effective Curriculum Management: Co-ordinating Learning in the Primary School*. London: Routledge.
Gardner, H. (1993) *Multiple Intelligences: The Theory in Practice*. New York: Basic Books.
Garratt, B. (1987) *The Learning Organisation*. London: Fontana/Collins.
Gipps, C. and Stobart, G. (1993) *Assessment: A Teacher's Guide to the Issues*. London: Hodder and Stoughton.
Graham, D. (1993) *A Lesson for Us All: The Making of the National Curriculum*. London: Routledge.
Handy, C. (1985) *Understanding Organisations*, 3rd edn. London: Penguin.
Hargreaves, D. H. (1995) School culture, school effectiveness and school improvement. *School Effectiveness and School Improvement*, 6(1): 23–46.
Harland, J. (1990) *The Work and Impact of Advisory Teachers*. Slough: NFER.
Harrison, B. and Mannion, K. (1998) Building scientific capability for the new millenium – the Pupil Researcher Initiative experience. *Education in Science*, April (177): 10–11.
Harrison, M. (ed.) (1995) *Developing a Leadership Role in Key Stage 2 Curriculum*. London: Falmer Press.
Honey, P. and Mumford, A. (1986) *The Manual of Learning Styles*, 2nd edn. Maidenhead: P. Honey.
Hopkins, D., Ainscow, M. and West, M. (1994) *School Improvement in an Era of Change*. London: Cassell.
Joyce, B. and Showers, B. (1980) Improving inservice training: the messages of research. *Educational Leadership*, February: 379–85.
Kelly, A. V. (1977) *The Curriculum: Theory and Practice*. London: Harper & Row Publishers.
Kerr, J. F. (ed.) (1968) *Changing the Curriculum*. London: University of London Press.
Kinder, K. and Harland, J. (1991) *The Impact of INSET: The Case of Primary Science*. Slough: NFER.
Knight, B. (1993) *Financial Management for Schools*. London: Heinemann.
Kolb, D. (1976) *Learning Style Inventory: Technical Manual*. Boston, MA: McBer & Co.
Kolb, D. (1984) *Experiential Learning: Experience as the Source of Learning and Development*, 2nd edn. Englewood Cliffs, NJ: Prentice Hall.
Lewis, A. (1995) *Primary Special Needs and the National Curriculum*, 2nd edn. London: Routledge.
Lewis, A. (1996) Assessment, in B. Carpenter, R. Ashdown and K. Bovair (eds) *Enabling Access: Effective Teaching and Learning for Pupils with Learning Difficulties*. London: David Fulton.
MacGilchrist, B., Mortimore, P., Savage, J. and Beresford, C. (1995) *Planning Matters*. London: Paul Chapman Publishing.
MacGilchrist, B., Myers, K. and Reed, J. (1997) *The Intelligent School*. London: Paul Chapman.

Ministry of Education (1959) *Primary Education: Suggestions for the Consideration of Teachers and Others Concerned with the Work of Primary Schools*. London: HMSO.

Moore, J. (1992a) The role of the science co-ordinator in primary schools. A survey of headteachers' views. *School Organisation*, 12(1): 7–17.

Moore, J. (1992b) Science co-ordinators in primary schools: the views of classroom teachers. *Education 3–13*, June: 33–7.

Morrison, K. (1986) Primary school subjects specialists as agents of school-based curriculum change. *School Organisation*, 6(2): 175–83.

Mortimore, P. (1997) Foreword, in B. MacGilchrist, K. Myers, and J. Reed, *The Intelligent School*. London: Paul Chapman Publishing Limited.

National Association of Governors and Managers (NAGM) (1994) *Visiting the School*, Paper 43. Birmingham: NAGM.

National Curriculum Council (NCC) (1989) *A Framework for the primary curriculum*. York: NCC.

National Council for Educational Technology (NCET) (1989) *Working with Teachers*. Coventry: National Council for Educational Technology.

Nias, J., Southworth, G. and Yeomans, R. (1989) *Staff Relationships in the Primary School: A Study of Organisational Cultures*. London: Cassell.

Nias, J., Southworth, G. and Campbell, P. (1992) *Whole School Curriculum Development in Primary Schools*. London: Falmer Press.

Novak, J. and Gowin, D. (1984) *Learning How to Learn*. Cambridge: Cambridge University Press.

Nuffield Primary Science (1995) *22 Teachers' Guides and 33 Pupils' Books*. London: Collins Educational.

Office for Standards in Education (Ofsted) (1993) *Handbook for the Inspection of Schools*. London: HMSO.

Office for Standards in Education (Ofsted) (1994) *Primary Matters*. London: HMSO.

Office for Standards in Education (Ofsted) (1995a) *Framework for the Inspection of Schools*. London: HMSO.

Office for Standards in Education (Ofsted) (1995b) *Science: A Review of Inspection Findings 1993/94*. London: HMSO.

Office for Standards in Education (Ofsted) (1996a) *Subjects and standards, Key Stages 1 & 2*. London: HMSO.

Office for Standards in Education (Ofsted) (1996b) *Primary Subject Guidance*. London: Ofsted.

Ollerenshaw, C. and Ritchie, R. (1997) *Primary Science: Making it Work*, 2nd edn. London: David Fulton Publishers.

O'Neill, J. (1996) Conclusion: co-ordinating teaching or learning?, in J. O'Neill and N. Kitson (eds) *Effective Curriculum Management: Co-ordinating Learning in the Primary School*. London: Routledge.

O' Neill, J. and Kitson, N. (eds) (1996) *Effective Curriculum Management: Co-ordinating Learning in the Primary School*. London: Routledge.

Osborn, M. and Black, E. (1994) *Developing the National Curriculum at Key Stage 2: The Changing Nature of Teachers' Work*, report commissioned by NAS/UWT. Bristol: University of Bristol.

Pollard, A. and Tann, S. (1987) *Reflective Teaching in the Primary School*. London: Cassell Education.

Porter, J. (1996) Issues in teacher training, in B. Carpenter, R. Ashdown, and K. Bovair (eds) *Enabling Access: Effective Teaching and Learning for Pupils with Learning Difficulties*. London: David Fulton.

Qualifications and Curriculum Authority (QCA) (1998a) *A Scheme of Work for Key Stages 1 and 2: Science*. London: DfEE.
Qualifications and Curriculum Authority (QCA) (1998b) *Key Stage 1, 1999 Assessment and Reporting Arrangements: Years 1 and 2, and Reception*. London: DfEE.
Qualifications and Curriculum Authority (QCA) (1998c) *Key Stage 2, 1999 Assessment and Reporting Arrangements: Years 3 to 6*. London: DfEE.
Reynolds, D., Bollen, R., Creemers, B., Hopkins, D., Stoll, L. and Lagerweij, N. (1996) *Making Good Schools: Linking School Effectiveness and School Improvement*. London: Routledge.
Ritchie, R. (ed.) (1991) *Profiling in Primary Schools: A Handbook for Teachers*. London: Cassell Education.
Ritchie, R. (1993) An evaluation of a practitioner's approach to the initial and inservice education of teachers in primary science based upon a constructivist view of learning. Unpublished PhD thesis, University of Bath.
Ritchie, R. (1995a) *Primary Design and Technology: a Process for Learning*. London: David Fulton Publishers.
Ritchie, R. (1995b) *Primary Science: Making it Work*. London: David Fulton Publishers.
Ritchie, R. (1996) Science, in B. Carpenter, R. Ashdown and K. Bovair (eds) *Enabling Access: Effective Teaching and Learning for Pupils with Learning Difficulties*. London: David Fulton.
Ritchie, R. (1997a) *The subject co-ordinator's role and responsibilities in primary schools*. Proceedings of the 3rd Primary Science Conference, Durham University, July.
Ritchie, R. (1997b) Assessment and recording as a constructive process, in A. Cross and G. Peet (eds) *Teaching Science in the Primary School: Book One, A Practical Source Book of Teaching Strategies*. Plymouth: Northcote House.
Sammons, P., Hillman, J. and Mortimore, P. (1995) *Key Characteristics of Effective Schools: A Review of School Effectiveness Research*. Report commissioned by the Office for Standards in Education. London: Institute of Education and Office for Standards in Education.
Schön, D. (1983) *The Reflective Practitioner: How Professionals Think in Action*. London: Maurice Temple Smith Ltd.
School Curriculum and Assessment Authority (SCAA) (1995) *Planning the Curriculum at Key Stages 1 and 2*. London: SCAA.
Sergiovanni, T. and Corbally, J. (eds) (1984) *Administrative Theory and Practice*. Urbana, IL: University of Illinois Press.
Skelton, J. (1996) Primary school co-ordinators: are they trained for leadership? *Inservice and Professional Development Association (IPDA) Newletter,* Spring.
Solomon, J. (1991) *School Home Investigations in Primary Science Book 1*. Hatfield: Association for Science Education.
Solomon, J. (1992a) *School Home Investigations in Primary Science Book 2*. Hatfield: Association for Science Education.
Solomon, J. (1992b) *School Home Investigations in Primary Science Book 3*. Hatfield: Association for Science Education.
Southworth, G. (1994) The learning school, in P. Ribbins and E. Burridge (eds) *Improving Education: Promoting Quality in Schools*. London, Cassell.
Southworth, G. (1995) *Looking into Primary Headship: A Research Based Interpretation*. London: Falmer Press.
Southworth, G. (1996) Improving primary schools: shifting the emphasis and clarifying the focus. *School Organisation*, 16(3): 263–80.
Stow, M. (1989) *Managing Mathematics in the Primary School – a Practical Resource for the Co-ordinator*. Windsor: NFER-NELSON.

Stow, M. and Foxman, D. (1988) *Mathematics Co-ordination: A Study of Practice in Primary and Middle Schools*. Windsor: NFER-NELSON.

Taylor, P. H. (1986) *Expertise and the Primary School Teacher*. Windsor: NFER-NELSON.

Teacher Training Agency (TTA) (1997) *Career Entry Profiles for Newly Qualified Teachers*. London: TTA.

Teacher Training Agency (TTA) (1998a) *National Standards for Subject Leaders*. London: TTA.

Teacher Training Agency (TTA) (1998b) *Needs Assessment Materials for Key Stage 2 Teachers: Assessing Your Needs in Literacy Mathematics and Science*. London: TTA.

Teacher Training Agency (TTA) (1998c) *Teacher Research Grants Scheme 1998: Applications for Research Grants*. London: TTA.

Times Educational Supplement (TES) (1989) Task Force. 15 December, p. 20.

Underwood, J. (1996) Co-ordinating information technology in the primary school, in J. O'Neill and N. Kitson (eds) *Effective Curriculum Management: Co-ordinating Learning in the Primary School*. London: Routledge.

Waters, M. (1996) *Curriculum Co-ordinators in Primary Schools*. London: Collins Educational.

Webb, R. and Vulliamy, G. (1995) The changing role of the primary school curriculum co-ordinator. *The Curriculum Journal*, 6(1): 29–45.

Webb, R. and Vulliamy, G. (1996) *Roles and Responsibilities in the Primary School*. Buckingham: Open University Press.

West, N. (1995) *Middle Management in the Primary School*. London: David Fulton.

West, N. (1996) Subject co-ordinators: they can't make it alone. *Managing Schools Today*. March: 18–20.

West-Burnham, J. (1996) Quality and the primary school curriculum, in J. O'Neill and N. Kitson (eds) (1996) *Effective Curriculum Management: Co-ordinating Learning in the Primary School*. London: Routledge.

Whitaker, P. (1993) *Managing Change in Schools*. Buckingham: Open University Press.

White, R. and Gunstone, R. (1992) *Probing Understanding*. London: Falmer Press.

Whitehead, J. (1989) How do we improve research-based professionalism in education? *British Educational Research Journal*, 15(1): 3–15.

Whiteside, T. (1996) The role of the co-ordinator auditing for development, in J. O'Neill and N. Kitson (eds) *Effective Curriculum Management: Co-ordinating Learning in the Primary School*. London: Routledge.

Wilson, L. and Eason, P. (1995) 'Teacher needs' and practice development. *British Journal of In-service Education*, 21(3): 273–84.

Young, T. L. (1997) Leading projects, in M. Preedy, R. Glatter and R. Levacic (eds) *Educational Management: Strategy, Quality and Resources*. Buckingham: Open University Press.

INDEX